For Timmy

I was blessed with forty-seven years of you in my life, during which time I faced unimaginable heartbreak. I channeled that heartbreak into strength, not just for myself, but for you. Had I the ability to take your pain, if only for a day, I'd have done so gladly. For, what you have given me is a lifetime of love, strength, and lessons in perseverance. To my hero, Timmy, I dedicate this book.

Table of contents

Foreword

Life's never been easy for M. Kate McNally. She's the youngest of seven children and the only daughter. She's the sole sister of six older brothers raised in a sibling dynamic that more often resembled a dog pack than a family. She grew up in a boy's camp that evolved (devolved?) into a raucous fraternity as children became teens. It was survival of the fittest and an endless struggle to gain attention, or avoid it, as the situation warranted. M. Kate McNally figured it out. While using many of the exclusive protections she possessed as a benefit of being dad's baby girl, she quickly developed a steely toughness that enabled her to adapt, survive, and thrive among all those brothers. Years later, that toughness manifested in a courageous and powerful force that gathered up and carried those brothers and their mom through a period of unimaginable heartbreak and sadness to a place of clarity, acceptance, peace—and love.

I know these things because M. Kate McNally is my sister. She's Mary Kate to my brothers and me. I'm the fourth child—the middle one—and Mary Kate will always be my baby sister. We were raised in a traditional Irish Catholic family in Easton, Pennsylvania, where Dad was an economist and business manager for a local cement company and Mom held the fort at home, attempting to manage what was often unmanageable. Family life meant Mass and mandatory Sunday dinner.

Days were filled with hectic schedules, homework struggles, tantrums, music and art lessons, baseball, basketball, football, softball, violent brotherly brawls, and awkward peace agreements. There were magical holidays, fear of Dad's punishments, and the comfort of Mom's unshakable faith in God and immeasurable love for us, regularly displayed with hugs so intense and comforting, they seemed capable of fixing everything in the world. Throughout my family's story, from its wonderful highs to its tragic lows, we were taught how to be dearly loved—and how to love dearly. Mary Kate learned those lessons well.

As I've watched Mary Kate write, speak, counsel and console in the years since our brother's death, I've been struck by the balance she maintains between the toughness she developed growing up as the youngest and only girl in our distinctly "boys" home, and her boundless capacity to demonstrate love in words, certainly—but mostly in deeds. It's love that drives her dogged persistence and dedication to the mission of erasing the stigma of mental illness and fostering important, lifesaving conversations about an extraordinarily painful subject. It's love that compels her to assist and comfort those who are struggling to care for their afflicted loved ones. It's love that fills her with the spirit to tell my brother's and my family's tragic, but hopeful, story in *How's Timothy?*

Yes, Timothy: my dear, sweet brother. We were brothers who became best friends. We spent our younger years as if in some idyllic kids' fantasyland, delivering newspapers, running off to baseball practice, sneaking into Lafayette College football games—and laughing together, always laughing together. As we grew into our twenties, I hired Timmy to work for me at the beer store I managed. Timmy was my best man and godfather to my first born, Andrew. We confided in each other and never doubted each other's trust. We enjoyed gatherings with my fledgling family and rock concerts and shared a passion for The Grateful Dead. I assumed Timmy would always be my kids' cool uncle and we'd always be best friends. And then it stopped.

In this labor of love, Mary Kate describes what she witnessed from very close range. She details the lessons learned—many the hard way—in attempting to compassionately care for a loved one with profound mental illness and a terminal disease. Mary Kate was no mere observer in this story. She was Timmy's voice and our family's de facto leader for all aspects of Timmy's care. She promised him she'd be his advocate until the end. He loved her deeply and trusted her implicitly with his life and what remained of it. My family and I trusted her, too. She held Timmy's hand from the time of his tragic diagnosis, through several extraordinarily difficult decisions regarding his treatment, and until the moment he drew his last breath. Mary Kate was no longer the baby of the family. She was its leader.

Mary Kate has important things to say in this book. She speaks from her personal experience, certainly. She also speaks for me and my family about telling Timmy's story and expressing our frustrations and struggles while trying to help him. Most importantly, she speaks for Timothy Thomas McNally, a beautiful soul whose life had immeasurable value and still does. It will be of immeasurable value to you if it simply increases your awareness and provides you the confidence and knowledge to speak up and seek help for yourself and others who are struggling with mental illness. You are not alone. My sister and my family have endured the worst and come through it with a greater love than we possessed when it started.

As I write these words, I am keenly aware that my pain has not eased much in the five years since Timmy's passing. I have tried not to discuss it, in an effort to protect myself from reopening wounds of regret and sadness about things I might have done differently for Timmy. I have written this foreword at the urging of my sister, who finally convinced me to speak and write about it. She has that kind of influence on me. I believe she will on you through the pages of this book.

Jim McNally

Author's brother

Chapter I
The Family

Dad. My dad grew up in Allentown, Pennsylvania, which was a small town when he was a kid. He lived for a time in Emmaus, but most of the stories I remember were from his time in Allentown. He was the youngest of three boys, although there was a fourth who died shortly after birth who would have been the oldest. Dad was a quiet man and extremely shy. His sense of humor was profound and dry, and one often had to pay close attention to realize he was joking. He and his brothers enlisted immediately when World War II was declared. Uncle James, the oldest, enlisted in the Army. Uncle John, the middle boy, joined the Air Force and my dad, the Navy. They joined under the G.I. Bill and were guaranteed college education once their time was served.

My dad often told the story of his brother John's death. My dad was in the South Pacific on a ship, transcribing Morse code, when he received his orders to return home for funeral leave. I'm not sure if he knew which brother had even been killed as the military is pretty hardened to such news and its delivery. Dad was devastated as he packed what he was able with such short notice. His thoughts turned to his mom and dad about whom he worried endlessly.

My dad returned home to say goodbye to his brother John. John's plane had gone down during routine formations. It had always been his

5

dream to be a fighter pilot and so he was. The viewing was held at my grandparents' house, which was customary during that time, as they had not started having viewings in the funeral home until years later. Guests would enter through the front door, pay their respects, and then leave through the back, cross over to the adjoining house, and exit through the neighbors'. John was only twenty-three. I can't begin to imagine my grandparents' horror, knowing they were now sending their remaining two sons back to war. Thankfully, they both returned home safely. The damage of having lost a son was enough to bear and surely took its toll on my grandmother, who they say never recovered from her loss and became sullen and withdrawn. The rest of the family struggled both to understand their loss and to remain strong for the sake of each other. My dad said that John always wanted to be a pilot and he died doing what he loved.

Uncle James, we were told, was a real prankster. He was the brother who, when the family would sit down to do a jigsaw puzzle together, would sneak off with one of the pieces only to emerge later as the guy who finished the puzzle. Uncle James once stood at the back of church, after his father's funeral, and shook hands with everyone, saying, "I'm so glad you met me." Just to prove that people really didn't listen. Apparently, my grandfather, the champion of the underdog also had a devilish sense of humor and loved pranks just as much as Uncle James. He had been in the hospital dying for some time when he chose the town drunk to be the undertaker for his funeral. When my grandfather passed away, the family honored his wish to have the funeral director of his choice handle the final arrangements. At the funeral, the director read from a book that he held upside down as he swayed back and forth in a drunken stupor. Amid all the mourning and tears, people were covering their faces to hide the laughter. My mom recalls Uncle Jim's shoulders shaking uncontrollably as he tried to stifle his laughing. Seems this was exactly what my grandfather would have wanted.

Unlike Uncle James, my dad was more innocent, yet still had the typical wry, Irish sense of humor. He was named after St. Francis of Assisi, and with his love for animals, that name could not have been more appropriate. Dad had several dogs throughout his childhood, and he intentionally mispronounced all their names. Perhaps as a rebellion against his mom, who never believed in nicknames. He once worked at a gas station that was going out of business because of financial problems, and when the owner had no money to pay my dad, he was told to take whatever he wanted. He took a few music records and the dog, to whom he had developed quite an attachment. There was never any need for a leash because the dog and my dad had become the best of friends and rarely left each other's sides.

One afternoon, my dad stopped by a candy store and the dog went in behind him. When the dog started helping himself to all the candy, my dad—perhaps not resembling St. Francis as much as we originally thought—left the store and pretended not to know whose dog it was. I believe that was Taurus, one of the only dogs to have his name pronounced properly. There was also Sagittarius, but my dad pronounced it Sag-a-tar-eus.

His love of dogs continued until the day he died. He rescued dog after dog, usually only one at a time until later in life when the house always had two. Dogs were treated like additional children; they never wanted for anything in his care.

Mom. My mom grew up in Philadelphia. My dad liked to tease her about this, saying, "Don't tell anyone and they'll never know." She was also the youngest of three and the daughter of Irish immigrants. Her parents had come to America separately and met once they had gotten established here. It was of utmost importance to both to become citizens as soon as they were able. My grandfather worked on the railroad and my grandmother was a maid for a wealthy French couple who became like family to her. They afforded her the opportunity to read from an extensive library where she found herself every moment she was able.

They were poor, and I mean poor. My mom tells about how exciting it was to find a piece of fruit in her stocking on Christmas morning. Imagine a kid today receiving a piece of fruit? The outrage! But to my mom and her brother and sister, it was a great blessing because they had so little.

My mom attended an all-girls school, Little Flower. I just recently found her class ring, which she told me I could keep because it no longer fit her. It doesn't fit any of my fingers either, but to have something that was so precious to her because of how poor her family was means a great deal to me. I love to hear her stories because they were such wonderful times for her and remind me how fortunate we are today. Because they were a family with only three children, the neighbors thought they were Protestant Irish. The Catholics, of course, had huge families. Although my grandmother was one of thirteen, she ended that cycle as far as her family was concerned, at least until my mom was married and...well.

Mom and dad. My parents met in Philadelphia after the war. My mom had been working for a ball bearing manufacturer doing secretarial work, and my dad took a job there after having finished graduate school at Temple University. Dad was a fantastic slow-pitch softball pitcher. He had invited my mom to come watch them play and I guess, as they say, the rest is history. It was a short courtship with the wedding on Thanksgiving Day and the feast as the reception dinner. It wasn't terribly long after that when my mom became pregnant with Mark.

"How can there be too many children? That is like saying there are too many flowers."

~Mother Teresa~

Mark. Son number one was Mark. Mark took his job as big brother seriously. Mark was shy but had a tremendous sense of humor, much like my dad. I always wondered if he felt bothered each time our mom brought another baby home, but if he was bothered by it, he never let on. He protected each and every one of us. He had a quick wit and a short temper. It didn't take much to anger him to the point of putting one of the brothers through a wall. Steve's teasing me into a screaming fit was one instance when Mark lost his cool. I remember him jacking Steve up against a wall, Steve's head denting the plaster, because the teasing had gotten out of hand and Mark just wanted to sleep. Mark often cleaned up messy situations that the brothers caused—usually Jimmy, going in with a puffed chest and then being unable to complete the task because of his small stature. Mark was extremely quiet, but he was also quite a presence. Mark was my godfather, a job he took quite seriously. It meant a little extra gift for Christmas or attention when I needed it. I was always grateful for that. I remember a few times being carried home from the park, thrown over Mark's shoulder because I had been stung by a bee or had acquired some other minor injury that seemed major to me. He never failed to show up just when I needed him.

One Easter, I got a new basketball, a favor for a tomboy such as myself. I headed towards the playground at the end of the street to break it in when a car full of older boys pulled up. They told me to get off the court because they were having a game. Being the stubborn little girl I was, I wouldn't budge, so they took my ball, threw it into the baseball field, and then one of them urinated on it. I guess he didn't know that I had six older, incredibly protective brothers only three houses away. I ran home to tell the boys and within seconds my six brothers were on the court with Mark in front. He grabbed the kid who threw the ball and peed on it and said, "Go get the ball, right now." The kid went and got it. When he returned, Mark pulled the kids shirt off and said, "Now, clean it off." He did as he was told after which Mark said, "Now, give the ball back to my sister, apologize, and get the hell out of here. And don't let me ever catch you in this park again." I got a sincere apology, after which they left, and I don't believe I ever saw them at the park again.

Steve. Steve was son number two. Steve was kind of the class clown of the family. He was notorious for prank phone calls and overall silliness. He was not only the class clown in the family but at school as well. Even the principal grew to appreciate Steve's silly phone calls. Steve would call the school office during morning announcements and, in a voice only Steve could do, tell the principal he was a "very bad man." Everyone in the school could hear the phone ringing in the background and they all knew it was Steve. Steve is also well known on a local radio station. His calls didn't necessarily make any sense, but they were so incredibly funny that the DJ tried to keep him on the phone.

Steve called, said what he had to say, and hung up quickly. He did show up once to meet the DJ, but he was wearing a mask so no one would know who he was.

Steve once worked for a landscaper, and at the time he drove a huge, old, beat-up Ford Fury that backfired regularly. Visible in the backseat, were jammed a wheelbarrow, shovels, and all the things one might see in the back of a pickup truck. He really didn't care what people thought of him as long as they laughed.

As we got older, we were sent out of the house every Sunday to go to church. One Sunday, while we were driving through the campus of Lafayette College, they were holding their graduation ceremony in the quad (a courtyard in the center of campus). The campus was filled with expensive cars, parents with fine suits and ties—you know, high-class stuff. Well, here comes Steve and his old Fury, backfiring, with Timmy, the youngest brother who was just in his early teens, in the passenger seat. Steve couldn't resist. He rolled down the windows and started yelling, as if he were a parent, at Timmy. "Why the hell are you not graduating with your class, Goddammit?" Timmy sat slumped down in the passenger seat holding back his laughter. All the while, the car was backfiring. Parents stopped in their tracks and stared, speechless. Steve never passed up an opportunity for a good laugh.

John. Son number three is John. The one who did enough worrying for all of us. John seemed very serious, but in truth he was just a big teddy bear with an undying sense of humor. His loyalty to the family was beyond measure and his heart was bigger than this world. John was the one my son, Sean, grew the closest to. John often referred to himself as uncle Buck, from the movie in which John Goodman plays the gambling, cigar smoking, and beer drinking uncle, which fit John perfectly. John was the one responsible for naming our dog, Apollo. It was 1969 when we got the dog, and the space shuttle had just landed on the moon, so he was named after the shuttle, which was, of course, the biggest news event of that year. John was also very protective. One night I pestered him into going to see a band I liked. While we were there, a guy he worked with showed up. The guy was known for abusing all the women he had ever dated. He was an alcoholic who hadn't sought help yet and was, at the time, an all-around crappy guy. He asked John, "Hey, would it be okay if I asked your sister to dance?" John answered, "Hey, would it be okay if I broke your fucking jaw?" That was that.

When I worked at a local tavern, John would come in after work for a beer. We had many of the same friends and never ran out of stories. We would share stories over a few beers, poking fun at the customers I waited on but mostly feeling a warmth towards the good souls we met. Sadly, as the story for bartenders goes, we attended many funerals together, as certain levels of alcoholism often have such sad endings.

Jimmy. Son number four was Jimmy. Jimmy was little but mighty. He was the one Mark usually had to save from a fight. Jimmy was an action taker. No sooner did an idea come into his mind than he was acting on it. He once sat in the shopping cart while at the store with our mom, asking people, "Aren't I so little and cute?" He wasn't one of the shy ones. As far as being protective, yes, he was another. I remember him saying he was going to ward off a stalker of mine with a nine-iron golf club. Jimmy was the closest with Timmy and they were friends through and through. Concerts, parties, work: they did everything together.

One night, on my way home from work at the bar, my car stalled. About seven college students were crossing in front of me, giving me the finger and making lewd gestures. The car started and I, of course, flipped out. Beeping the horn, yelling, etc., and then the car stalled again. The gang of guys came back and now jumped on the car. One was on the roof; two were on the hood, kicking the windshield; and the others surrounded the car, kicking it. I was in a panic and, thankfully, the car started. Again, my mighty Irish temper arose, and I flipped out for a second time. This vicious cycle went on for yet another round. Finally, the car started for good, and I was able to get home. By this time, I was visibly shaken. Jimmy grabbed a baseball bat and said, "Come with me." We went to Wawa, a local convenience store known mostly to Pennsylvanians, where the guys were heading. When we got there the manager was preparing to close the store because the guys had come in and urinated on all the shelves and destroyed the place. Thankfully for everyone, they were gone. Jimmy would probably be in jail to this day had he caught them. This was typical of him. No one was going mess with me or any other family member and get away with it.

Dennis. Son number five was Dennis. Dennis and Timmy were Irish twins, born within eleven months of each other. For one week each December, they were the same age. Dennis and Tim were really close as kids. Dennis always felt responsible for making sure that Timmy was paying attention to the rules and would enforce them with strict punishment when he broke them. The punishment was usually a bite on the arm, but it always worked. Dennis was the mastermind behind the elaborate alarm system we used to determine when my parents went to bed on Christmas Eve so we could sneak downstairs and get an early look at what we were all getting. The system was composed of a string that ran the length of the hallway from my parents' bedroom to Dennis' room. When the door to my parent's room closed, the string would vibrate, ringing a bell that was in Dennis' room, alerting us that they had gone to bed. Dennis had cut thick Styrofoam in the shape of his shoes and used rubber bands to fasten them to his feet so he could walk more stealthily and not be heard going downstairs. Timmy and I were brave; we just went down and took our chances. It paid off because we were never caught.

Dennis was also very shy. He kept to himself unless he was with the family. We were never terribly close, but he worried anytime something was going on with me. If I had been sick, he would repeatedly ask Mom how I was. Dennis and I were never close, but we seemed to have a mutual caring deep down. Once, Dennis bought a Saab that I had to drive home from the dealership for him because it was a manual, and then I taught him how to drive a stick. I was about three months pregnant with my son at the time. Years later, he bought another Saab and literally gave me the old one. It was in pristine condition and it was my pride and joy for many years after that.

Timmy. The youngest boy and son number six, about whom this book is written. I came four years later, much to Tim's chagrin. He did get over it in time, and we became great friends. We were sort of forced together because we were both so young. I remember hearing stories about the boys complaining that they wouldn't be allowed to walk around in the house in their underwear anymore now that there was a girl there. Seems a lot of things had to change once I arrived. My dad went from using black-and-white film to using color. That was huge. We remark today that the boys were only worthy of black-and-white film, but the coup de grace, the little girl, was worthy of color film. I got away with a lot, with my dad saying, "She's just a little girl." It's a wonder the brothers loved me after all that! But they did. They would tease the daylights out of me and then turn around and nearly kill someone outside the family for picking on me. That's just the way it worked.

Me. Mrs. McNally finally had a girl. It was touch and go for my first few days with blood transfusions, emergency baptism and confirmation, final blessings, and my mom's being told that she might not be taking this one home. She was heartbroken. Suddenly, at about two in the morning, the pediatrician rushed to the hospital after having figured out what was wrong. Back then, little was known about Rh factor. I had my dad's O negative and my mom's B positive blood coursing through me, and they were causing one hell of an uproar. Dr. Parry figured it out, and that is when I had the whole blood transfusion, making me 100 percent O negative. In addition, it was discovered I had a severe allergy to milk. With all these pieces figured out, I was able to go home. Little did I know what lay in store.

Apollo (the dog). It was 1969 and John wanted a dog. After having had many cats, hamsters, gerbils, and guinea pigs, it was decided that John could have a dog. No one in the house was adept at training a dog. My dad had dogs when he was a kid, but I don't think anyone knew how to properly train one. Our next-door neighbor, who is much like a grandmother to us, had a daughter whose dog had just had puppies. Apparently, the mother had been hit by a fire truck and had immediately given birth. By the time our family made the decision to take a puppy, all of them had been adopted except for Apollo. It didn't take a lot of thought; we took him.

Apollo was aptly named after the Apollo 11 moon landing that was happening the year he was born. He was an unusual looking dog. As the veterinarian said, he had a lot of ancestors. I was only a year old, so Apollo and I grew up together. He once saved me from certain death when he grabbed the back of my pants with his teeth just as I was about to go headfirst down the basement steps. He was fiercely loyal and protective, but he lacked manners. He once walked up to a little boy at the playground and took candy right out of his hand. This pretty much summed up who Apollo was. He was, as my mom always described him, a junkyard dog. He was once tied to a cinderblock to keep him from chasing cars. This didn't stop him; he ran down the street dragging the cinderblock behind him.

Cleaning day was always interesting as my mom would pull the couch out to clean behind it and she would always find empty pizza boxes, candy wrappers, beer cans, and sometimes dirty silverware. It was as if Apollo had his own bachelor pad. He didn't seem to mind if my mom cleaned up after him, but if she dared to reprimand him, he would show his teeth as if to say, "You can clean it up, but don't give me any flack about it, lady." The words, "Did you do that?" Said in just the right tone released the monster that lived inside our dog. As years went on, all you had to do was use the acronym D.Y.D.T. in an angry tone and it had the same effect. John started saying, "Yabba dabba dooo." It was the tone of voice Apollo understood, but we like to think that he knew what we were saying. He didn't take kindly to being punished. He was as tough as nails and feared nothing. The only thing that humbled him was being wet. He would play in the snow and have a great time for hours, but once he was inside, he would literally go stand with his face in the corner, ashamed at how wet he was. The only time when this meant something other than shame was after a bath. All the furniture that was off-limits to him was now fair game. My mom had antique furniture that he was not allowed to go on. So, after a bath, in a thumbing-his-nose fashion, he would jump on each and every piece of antique furniture. We assumed he was saying, "There, now we're even, assholes."

Every summer, the playground a few houses down had a teenager who led activities and oversaw play. There was a large shed filled with games, balls of every kind—basketball, baseball, kickball, football, tennis, knock hockey—coloring books, and crayons. We would spend hours there every day and only go home when we were called. One of the activities was a dog pageant. All the kids would bring their dogs and display whatever special talents they had. Apollo had no real talent and he didn't play well with other dogs, so an exception was made, and the judges would come to the house to judge Apollo. He always won "most unique." Well, he certainly was that.

There were a few occasions when one of the brothers would be locked out of the house. This was rare because up until a few years ago I didn't know the doors even had locks, or keys. All the boys were skilled climbers. Some climbed out when they were grounded and others climbed in if it happened to be a rare occasion when the door was locked. Apollo was usually asleep on someone's bed, but on the night Jimmy decided to climb in the front bedroom window, Apollo was asleep on the bed that was against that window. I'm happy to report that Jimmy still has his right leg. I guess that even if Apollo knew who you were, if you weren't entering the house through anything other than the front door, you were fair game. He also took exception to being moved when he was asleep. It was not unusual to return from the bathroom in the middle of the night to find that Apollo had moved up and taken over your pillow. I spent quite a few nights sleeping at the foot of the bed to avoid the growling monster I would encounter should I try to move him.

A story not well known by my parents, or even discussed much since it happened, was the day Apollo found a bag of marijuana. Yes, he ate the whole thing and was stoned out of his mind. He was falling over and walking into things. We were all scared to death because we had no idea he had eaten pot. We thought he got into rat poison in the woods or at the park or something. The dog had survived so many crazy things like being hit by a car, and now this? We rushed into our vet who pumped his stomach. I believe he sent us off with a warning that Apollo may have the munchies in a few hours. We never told my parents what was in his stomach. That would mean ratting out one of the brothers, who I still won't call out.

Chapter II
Growing Up McNally

"You call it chaos; we call it family."
P. Graham Dunn

Together. We grew up in a small town in Pennsylvania on a one block street with a beautiful playground at the end of the road. That was precisely why my dad had chosen this house. There were already three McNally boys when he bought the house, and mom was pregnant with number four. The playground had a nice-sized baseball field framed by a wooded area and a stream that carried water from the city pumping station that sat at the top of the hill on the same property. The stream was famous for salamanders and mica rocks that we pretended were silver. There was no need to run home for water as the water in the stream was always ice cold and we drank it regularly. I imagine that today that would be viewed the same as drinking from the garden hose, yet we all managed to survive.

The woods were a favorite for all age groups. There was a fort back there for many years. It was deserted by each generation as they reached high school. It would then be taken over by the next, younger group. Many days were spent hiking through those woods. The stories are endless. One summer, the kids attached a rope swing but there was no water in which to land, just a rock to launch from and return to for landing. The big story that summer wasn't the rope swing; it was the neighbor up the street who fell from several feet up and broke both arms and legs. She spent the summer watching the world from a wheelchair on her front porch. No one used the rope swing ever again after that.

In the late '60s and throughout the '70s, most families had only one car and the father used it to go to work, leaving the street empty. We had the blue Comet station wagon, which became a bit of a legend. The car of choice back in the late '60s and early '70s, for large families, was the station wagon. We had a few throughout my childhood, but the Comet was priceless. It was a faded blue, like an old fence needing paint. It had no seatbelts, a bench seat that sat three across the front, and those little corner windows that had their own cranks. We liked to sit in what we called "the way back," which was the wagon portion of the station wagon. Some of the newer cars had a seat back there, but not ours. We sat, hanging out the rear window, facing traffic. When I was just a baby, there was no need for fancy car seats, not when Mom had a perfectly good lap on which to sit. And airbags? No such thing. I suppose the lower number of cars on the road and lack of speed made the roads quite a bit safer; therefore, seatbelts were never required.

One summer evening, just after dinner, Mark was waiting to go to his guitar lesson. Mark was a man of few words, and he didn't express excitement in any form. He was the brother who often covered his mouth when he laughed, almost as if he feared someone might catch on that he had a sense of humor. That night, Mark left for his lesson and returned just as quickly, with guitar still in hand. He slowly approached Mom in the kitchen and said, "I think you may want to call the fire department." There was no 911 back then. You had emergency phone numbers kept by the phone or you could dial zero for the operator.

"What for?" asked Mom.

"Well," Mark said, "it appears that the car is on fire." He probably remained calm so that she would too, but that never worked—she panicked at the word fire. Our next-door neighbor was a policeman. She knew he would hear the call over the radio, and my mom was already embarrassed enough. She asked the person on the phone to please send just a small truck. "No need for the hook and ladder," she added. She asked that they not sound sirens either. "Just one truck will be necessary," she said.

The person on the phone asked, "Lady, what size truck do you want?" It really didn't matter. Our neighbor, the policeman, had heard the call and, being the owner of the other half of the double, the one connected to our house, he panicked and had every fire truck in the city sent. The sirens were blaring and the one-block-long street was flooded with fire trucks and police cars. Needless to say, they made quick work of extinguishing the car. As my mom feared, this led to question after question from the neighbors, who were, as anyone would be, concerned, yet she didn't want to talk about it, ever. In a few days, the tow truck would come to take the old beast a away. Every kid in the neighborhood lined our steps to bid farewell as she was taken on her final journey, attached to the back of a tow truck.

Although we had the playground, we often played in the street. Our favorite was a game we called "bounce off." It required two people. One bounced the ball off the steps while the other stood on the other side of the street and fielded the ball. It was a rare occasion to have a car come through the street, so we could play that game for hours. We always joked that if you drove down our street, you lived there, were visiting, or you were lost. From very early in the morning until well after the sun went down, you could hear the kids playing outside. As I said, these were simpler times; *innocence* is the word that comes to mind. This was back when neighbors knew each other, and moms helped each other with the kids. It wasn't unusual for Mom to receive a phone call telling her that one of the boys was doing something he wasn't supposed to be doing. The woman across the street couldn't keep track of all the names, so she called the boys by number. One day, Mom answered a frantic phone call from the very woman, who could barely form the words to tell her that sons number three and four were walking across the spouting outside the third floor, along with my grandfather who had turned his hearing aid off. We lived in a five-bedroom, Victorian house that sat on top of a steep bank. Any fall from the third floor would've been deadly. The boys sure kept our mom busy.

Through it all, we grew to be a very close family. My dad's goal was to have his kids look out for each other, and we all did. We fought like a bunch of Irishmen, but we had each other's backs no matter what.

Now that you know who all the characters are, I'll continue this story about a beautiful soul. The most beautiful soul I've ever known. I'm quite certain my heart will never heal, and I hope that it won't as it serves as my constant reminder of who Tim was, what he meant to me, and how telling his story may help another family. I promised Timmy a few things; one of them was to be his voice. And, being his voice, I decided to make sure everyone knows that Tim's life mattered. Tim's life still matters, as he is with all of us, in our hearts and in our thoughts every single day.

There is a part of Timmy's charisma and spirit in all of us—the family, that is. Timmy was different from the rest of us, but in such a unique and wonderful way. He was taller than the other boys, with lighter hair and a gorgeous, chiseled face like that of a model. You couldn't help but love him. Rich, my longtime boyfriend, once sent me an article about research that showed cells are left in the mother's body after childbirth. Some of those cells can then be passed on to the next children or many children. Those cells can pass on for generations. That may explain my overwhelming connection with Timmy. Although I was younger, I was always protective of him. If I could've placed him in a bubble where no one and nothing could ever hurt him, I would have. It's a feeling much like the one I have for my son. This love has no definition; it's unconditional, for certain.

Timmy and I were always close, even after he spent the first few years being jealous of my arrival. For four years, Timmy had been the baby of the family. He objected greatly to having to share my father's lap with me now. With so many kids in the family, each time one of us got up to get a drink or go to the bathroom, we called our seat saved. It came right down to calling my father's lap saved so no one would dare sit there if we had to get up for any reason. If anyone dared to take your seat after you called it saved, court would be held right there in front of the TV. Our mom and dad were often called as witnesses and asked to testify whether they heard us call the seat saved. One brother even went so far as to fart on the cushion, certain his territory had been marked and no one would dare to trespass. This was the cause of many fights in our house. After we learned to share the coveted seat, Timmy and I shared more than just my dad's lap. We shared a bond, a friendship, and a big brother-little sister connection that will surely stay with me for the rest of my life.

Dennis, M. Kate, Timmy, and Mom in back. M. Kate's First Holy Communion

We were a crazy Irish-Catholic family. All the boys took turns at being altar boys, and we all went to Catholic school. The days of altar boys were filled with great stories. Dennis and Tim were often assigned to the same mass, so they were a pair. They both wanted the duty of ringing the bells after the consecration of the host (blessing of the bread to make it represent the body of Christ) and would ring them emphatically when it was their turn, even after stern warnings from my parents. Church was always an adventure when we were little. Imagine my parents with seven kids, taking up an entire pew, strategically seating us to keep the troublemakers separated. There was poking going on behind their backs, faces being made, and kicking. I guess one would say we really needed church! My dad had all the boys dressed in brown pants and white shirts; they hated it. I always had on a dress. Funny thing is, as much as none of us wanted to go to church, we played "mass" when my parents went out. One of the brothers would be in charge of watching me, as a babysitter was never hired. One of us would take the oil and vinegar cruets, meant to represent the water and wine. Then, we smashed bread and cut it with a drinking glass to look like hosts for our communion, and Apollo would serve as altar boy for John, the priest. I think Mom's hair took on some new gray when she walked in to find John giving Apollo communion.

As we got older, we were responsible for getting ourselves to church if we didn't want to go with our parents. We could walk over to the chapel at Lafayette College or down to St. Michael's. For the brothers who drove, they could go to St. Bernard's or "St. McDonald's." The latter is where I usually went with Mark and Timmy. We would go, eat breakfast, over which we never prayed. It wasn't so much Catholic guilt we felt, but the threat of life and limb, if we ever spoke a word of this to the others. We would then drive by church, where I would run in to grab "a receipt" (a copy of the church bulletin) and see who the priest was. I always opted to go to "church" with Mark because he had money to buy "communion".

One Sunday, Mark had gone by himself, although I don't remember the details of why. When questioned at the dinner table, he said he had forgotten his bulletin and the priest was father Kulik. Mom dropped her fork and glared at him.

"Father Kulik was transferred two years ago."

Mark said, "Well, he was there visiting." Game over. Our mom knew everything that went on at that church and which priests were where. She surely would've known if Father Kulik was visiting. Sadly, "St. McDonald's" was no longer our parish.

Sunday dinner was a mandatory event each week. It was the one meal my dad expected everyone to attend. This was where we brought proof that we had been to church that morning—the bulletin and knowledge of which priest said the mass. Mom would make a roast beef with all the trimmings. She would set the table as if we were having fancy company, when actually it was just a bunch of savage boys and me. We identified each section of the table as if we were a town. We had the bad neighborhood, the classy section, and the dog under the table trick-or-treating.

One of my earliest memories of Sunday dinner was when I was young enough not to suffer consequences for most of my actions. My brothers were expected to behave like gentleman, and I sat, ensconced, between Mom and Dad. I remember the rumbling in my stomach becoming an audible belch. I, of course, failed to say excuse me. After all, as Dad reminded everyone regularly, I was just a little girl. Dennis, who sat in the slum neighborhood, protested. He demanded that I say excuse me, as he would never have gotten away with such behavior at the dinner table. He followed his demand by giving me the finger. I had no idea what it meant, so I returned the gesture. My parents hadn't seen him do it, but they saw me returning the favor. With no hesitation, I said I was only doing what he had done to me. Dennis was sent to his room, mumbling all the way up the stairs that Filth, his name for me, had belched and now he was being punished. Oh, the unfairness of it all! But, after all, I was just a little girl, and he did, in fact, give me the finger, which was a much more serious offense.

As far as school was concerned, my brothers' having gone before me was a blessing and a curse. The teachers seemed to have pretty low expectations as far as my conduct was concerned. I had some pretty big shoes to fill, yet I was a little too shy to carry out the same behaviors as my brothers. On the other hand, my brothers could give me pointers on how to handle certain teachers they had already dealt with. We had one teacher who regularly doled out punishment in the form of a yellow legal-size paper, numbered and lined, on which we were expected to write thirty-six times, "This assignment urges me to do what I should without being told." This was assigned if you hadn't handed in homework on time, had arrived late to class, or any other offense the teacher considered punishable. Given the number of times I had to do that assignment, I will never forget those words. Depending on the crime, the punishment could have been more than one of those sheets. Our little hands ached by the time we got to number 36. Timmy taught me that if I held two pens, I could get the job done in half the time. He spoke from experience and it saved me the pain and aggravation of truly completing the assignment. He was always crafty like that. He was funny, smart, creative, and downright good-looking! Timmy knew how to have fun and get away with anything and everything.

Jimmy was another pro when it came to "getting away with stuff." He had taught me that the reason our mom never let me do things is because I asked. He said, Just go do whatever it is you want to do. If you get caught, well, at least you got to go do what you wanted." A sort of ask-for-forgiveness rather than ask-for-permission. This worked well for me.

We had all become professionals at forging our mom's signature. I learned in first grade. While standing at the bus stop one day, I realized I had forgotten to have my mom sign a test that I had to hand back to the teacher that day. In tears, I pleaded with Jimmy to run home and have her sign it. He said not to worry as he grabbed a pen and did her signature almost better than she did. He advised that, for the future, I had better learn this too.

The funny thing about Timmy was he seemed shy. I sometimes look back in shock at the things he did because they all seemed out of character for him, but those were the things that made Timmy, well, Timmy. The last day of eighth grade was a big deal. It was the end of what was then considered elementary school. Next up was high school, and Timmy had been granted his wish to transfer out of Catholic school and attend the local public high school. So, on the last day, coming home on the bus, Timmy and his buddies sat in the last seat, which really didn't seem that unusual. When the bus was about six blocks from our stop, Timmy and his buddy threw a smoke bomb and jumped out the emergency door. The alarm sounded, the bus filled with smoke, and the driver went right into a panic. *What the hell just happened*, I thought. I looked out the window, and there was Timmy running down the street, laughing.

Timmy was the great improviser. The perfect example was his creativity when playing war. All the neighborhood kids got together and played war on most summer afternoons. Most of the kids had fancy guns that made noises and lit up as if they were firing. The McNally kids made guns out of sticks. We simulated noises as we were firing on our enemy—you know, typical gun sounds. Not Timmy, his gun made fart noises. It was hysterical. No one could ever mistake being shot by Timmy. Our life was good! We were in no way spoiled, but we never lacked love. We fought like true Irishmen but loved each other fiercely. As our teen years approached, we made new friends and found new hobbies. We all went our separate ways, but we always knew where home was.

A common ground for concern for all of us was always Timmy. There was a certain innocence about him that won hearts and broke hearts. I always looked at him as my cool older brother. He could play any sport like a pro, and he had cool clothes, cool friends, and cool music. Most of the music I listen to today is the same music Tim and I listened to as teenagers. One of my favorite things about Timmy was he always had time to hang out with me and didn't seem put off that I was his baby sister who was tagging along.

Our childhood was certainly memorable as we lived in a big house with five bedrooms, a nice big backyard, and the playground at the end of our block. We felt darned lucky. The playground, as I explained earlier, was a wonderland—with the baseball field, basketball court, and play area with sliding board and swings and a huge wooden teepee. From the time we woke up until the time our moms called us home at night, that's where most of us could be found. It didn't matter what stage of life we were going through, the park had something for all of us. My brothers could play baseball while my friends and I sat on the swings down below. In fact, this is how my best friend Marla and I became best friends. We were only infants, but our older brothers were good friends.

On days when they were supposed to be watching us, they would take us to the park, sit us in the middle of the baseball field, and then go play basketball. The field was big enough that there was no concern that we would get in trouble. Hell, I couldn't even walk yet. That was almost fifty years ago, and Marla and I are still inseparable.

The older boys often played poker on the teepee, a huge, open, wooden structure. After each game the little kids would crawl underneath to get all the change that the guys had dropped. That's the place where I drove them all crazy. They wanted to hang out, be cool with their friends, and smoke cigarettes. They surely didn't want their little sister hanging around. It was probably during that time when Timmy and I became even closer. Since we were the two youngest, we were often at home while the older boys went out. We didn't seem to mind, though; we always found things to do to entertain ourselves.

Chapter III

What Goes on in That House?

Saturday nights with Timmy are my favorite memories. We always had a blast. Our dad went to bed early, and our mom never failed to fall asleep on the couch. The (as my grandmother would have said) shenanigans started with the Saturday night television lineup: *The Love Boat* followed by *Fantasy Island*. Since the guests on the shows were often stars from other shows, Timmy and I insisted they be called the names they were on whatever show they were famous from. We made up our own storylines; Timmy could have been a screenwriter for how well he rewrote scripts for the shows we watched. What was meant to be drama, in Tim's hands, became a comedy. Eventually the fun and games moved into the kitchen, where we pretended to create culinary masterpieces. We usually made homemade potato chips in our FryDaddy (a home version deep fryer) or some type of salad that neither of us was ever interested in eating. Our dog Apollo, however, was more than happy to be our patron and eat everything we gave him. In retrospect, it's a small miracle we never burned that house down.

Once we had thoroughly destroyed the kitchen, it was time to make prank phone calls. Back then, there was no caller ID, no star 69, no way for anyone to know who was calling them. Timmy wrote in-depth scripts, we practiced them until everything was just right, and then we went to the phone book and picked unsuspecting targets. I called from our telephone in the hallway while Tim listened in on the kitchen phone. You could faintly hear his giggles in the background as I called such places as a Chinese restaurant downtown. I always used a very deep voice, so no one ever suspected a little girl on the other end of the phone. I pretended to place a take-out order, asking for shrimp fried rice. When they repeated the order back as "shimp fly lice," I said, "No, I don't want lice." They would then repeat the order back a second time, and each time I argued that I did not want lice. All that went on until they finally realized it was prank phone call and hung up on me. We thought we were hysterical and didn't, as kids, recognize how inappropriate this was. Had Mom been awake, we'd have been read the riot act on how racist our little prank was. The next script was often for a guy in our town who we decided was a pervert. He was known for watching girls at church and for driving to the high school parking lot to scope out the girls there. He was our favorite target. I called and told him how I had been watching him for some time and I thought he was really cute. I asked if we could meet somewhere, usually McDonald's. He always said yes. I never know if he showed up.

One evening, while our mom was asleep on the couch, Timmy made a bet with me he could make Mom slap herself in the face. I was insistent there was no way he could do that. Then he took a string, gently ran it across her nose and, sure enough, she smacked herself in the face! We tried so hard to sit still and act as if we had done nothing while she looked around to see what may have been crawling on her face. Every Saturday night, we did our best to stay awake until *Saturday Night Live* came on. We sat with our fingers crossed that the guest star would be Steve Martin. This was back in the day when they had the "Not Ready for Prime Time Players," the name of the group that made up the original cast. I'm sure it wasn't something Timmy and I should have been watching, but nobody ever knew. When Mom finally woke up, she shooed us off to bed. That was another adventure. Halfway up our staircase, there was a closet, and I was certain there were monsters in that closet. Timmy told me that the monsters would never come out if you farted when you walked past. I can't tell you how many times I walked up the steps making fart noises with my mouth to ensure my safe passage. I am certain Timmy was somewhere laughing at that. My God, he was funny!

For a time when we were little, Timmy and I shared a bedroom. We would lie awake and talk for hours at night. We went through the entire neighborhood, connecting the names of the pets with the families' last names. For example, our dog was Apollo McNally. We laughed while deciding what our children's names would be if we had different last names. Timmy always said if his last name was Case, he would name his son Justin.

Aside from the great times Timmy and I had, the boys always had something going on and I was rarely included, but I desperately wanted to be. For instance, the Dapper Dan club. The Johnson Smith catalog was a huge hit at our house and many of the pranks played by the Dapper Dan club came from this company. It was filled with all sorts of gags, such as gum that made your teeth turn black and a handshake buzzer to zap your friends unexpectedly. We never had a shortage of whoopee cushions at our house. Our mom would take them away and a new one would be in the mail just as quickly. Back in the '70s, one could easily place an order C.O.D. (cash on delivery). Dennis, the president of the Dapper Dan Club, was the collector of all things gross: fake vomit, fake dog poop, and anything slimy. He would mail in his order and then leave the money, likely in the form of loose change, with Mom. She would then pay the mailman for whatever disgusting thing he delivered Back to the Dapper Dan club. Dennis was the leader. If you were a boy, you were welcomed into the club with no initiation. I, however, had to earn it. I wanted so desperately to be in that club, although I'll never really remember why. I was told that I could earn my way into the club by retrieving the fake dog poop from the toilet. *Hell, that's easy*, I thought. I ran into the bathroom reached directly into the toilet and… Well, it wasn't the fake dog poop.

With such shenanigans, Christmas was not so much a holiday as it was an opportunity to try out some new invention that we'd cooked up. One year it was the foam shoes Dennis invented. Another was when Timmy and I snuck down at around four in the morning. We craftily opened each gift. Timmy would gently slide his finger under the tape and ever so delicately, lift it from the paper, being sure not to make the slightest tear. We played with all the new toys, and I tried on a new snowsuit that I had begged for. We were outside playing, in the house playing, and no one ever knew. Timmy was just as gifted at rewrapping as he took the same painstaking steps to be sure every piece of tape was exactly where it had been. There was no evidence of our early morning visit. Sadly, there was also no excitement for us when the others woke up Christmas morning. It was then that our acting skills were sharpened and really put to the test as we faked our *oohs* and *ahs*, with eyes wide. I think we did pretty well, considering our parents never seemed to catch on.

Since the family was so big, we had the Pollyanna, which was our version of a gift swap. After Thanksgiving dinner, each of us would pick two names from a dish. These would be the two people for whom you would buy gifts. My dad would help me because I was the baby of the family and clearly had no money. Each of us would write a list for the others, usually to be ignored when we bought whatever it was we felt like giving. I was lucky, though. Mark had a job, was my godfather, and almost always pulled my name. He always bought me something special and not from my list.

One year, I had pulled John's name. My dad and I carefully picked out just the right pillow for him. Yes, that was my gift to him, and I was certain that the others would be disappointed that I hadn't pulled their names. In the bursting enthusiasm of the seven-year-old, I exclaim to John about two weeks before Christmas, "You are going love the pillow I got you!" I then cried. He assured me that he would be surprised because he didn't know what it looked like. I accepted that and moved on. We opened the family gifts on Christmas Eve, starting with the youngest and working our way up. John acted surprised to receive the pillow he was expecting because, as he'd said, he didn't know what it looked like. I managed to dampen the mood right off the bat when I opened my Gnip Gnop from Jimmy. I let out a sigh, saying that I didn't really want this game. Clearly, I had not yet learned the art of tact.

Being the only girl with six older brothers, it was inevitable that I became a tomboy. I wanted all things baseball. I asked for a New York Yankees baseball uniform every year for as long as I can remember. I never did get one, damn Santa. He did bring me a Crissy doll, which was proof that Santa had no idea who I was. I had exactly zero dolls until that day. Perhaps this was a ploy to alter the field of influence from my brothers. An attempt to make me more "girly." After all, my parents had waited all these years for a daughter and now they had one who, in behavior, closely resembled all her brothers. Crissy was a doll with long hair. She had a button on her back that when turned, made her hair retreat inside her head, and then she had short hair. Another button on her belly, when pushed, allowed you to pull her hair back out of her head, and now she had long hair again. I imagine other "normal" girls probably had this at the very top of their Christmas list with stars and arrows bringing emphasis to this particular hot item. I, however, reserved that spot for the never-received baseball uniform. It was for that reason that I didn't mind my brothers "borrowing" Crissy to play a new game called "barbershop." Barbershop was a game where Crissy had her hair washed, in the toilet, and then cut off. When my father walked in on three of his sons standing over the toilet, holding a sopping wet Crissy doll with a horrific new haircut, the man who never raised his voice now had new veins protruding from his temples and neck, likely working to hold in all the things he wanted to yell. Remembering that I was just a little girl, my father spared me any punishment. That was the first and the last time barbershop was ever played.

Chapter IV
Things Are Changing

So, back to Timmy. I want to tell Timmy's story the best that I can. All that follows started out as a journal—my journal. My life has changed so much in forty-nine years, but all those changes seem somehow normal. This one event involving Timmy changed me forever. It caused me to question my faith in God, it shook all that I stood for, it made me quite literally question my place in this world. I see life as an incredible journey. I know and I understand that painful events must take place just as happy events take place. All of these things help us to grow and to make us whole. I experienced heartbreak when my father died after battling cancer. I experienced an even more devastating heartbreak when my oldest brother Mark was struck head-on and killed by an SUV while riding a motorcycle through the high desert of California. Neither of these, nor their combination, could match the unbearable heartbreak of what I faced with Timmy. That said, I have also experienced tremendous joy, the birth of my son being the most miraculous of those experiences. I was blessed with an incredible family. We were raised to be kind and caring. My dad was a firm believer in anonymously doing kind gestures. He said it only counts if you don't get caught. My dad was a good man and I like to think that we made him proud throughout the years.

Timmy was a great athlete. He played baseball and basketball and ran cross country as if he was born to do all these things. He once played tirelessly in a basketball league to see that his team got to the playoffs. During the last game of the season that year, Timmy had a fever of 102 yet scored more points than anyone on the team, leading them to the championship. He did well under pressure. He went through a time where he lifted weights, but I think that was to impress a girl. Twin girls had moved in next door to us, and they were beautiful. Timmy dated one and his friend from across the street, Jeff, dated the other. The one Timmy dated was Sara. I remember his loving the Hall & Oates song "Sara Smile." If I'm not mistaken, Hall & Oates played a concert nearby at the time. My memory fails me when it comes to how the relationship ended, but I do know that when that happened, Tim's friendship with Jeff also ended. I believe they both liked the same twin and things got a bit complicated.

As I approached my teen years, I established my own group of friends and Tim had his. One of Tim's best friends, Bob, was someone I will never forget. I try not to use the word hate, but it's the only word that comes to mind when I think of Bob. Timmy was seventeen and Bob was about thirty. He was a perpetual teenager. At one time or another, he hung out with each of my brothers. As they grew up and Bob didn't, they would move on and Bob would befriend the next McNally boy. He seemed cool to the younger kids because he carried a little satchel with pot and he could buy beer. There were likely other drugs, but I never had proof. There were many times I tried to convince Timmy not to hang out with him, to no avail.

41

One night, my friends and I were at a local corner store when we saw Tim with Bob. I was desperate to get Timmy away from him. I begged and pleaded with Timmy to come with me when Bob turned around and said, "Fuck her, let's go get high." I was heartbroken. You could see Timmy's confusion; he didn't know which way to go. He shrugged his shoulders and walked away with Bob. I believe he went out of fear. My brother Jim has a more forgiving memory of Bob, but as far as I'm concerned, he should have been charged with child abuse. How dare he put my brother in any kind of danger! It was during Tim's friendship with Bob that life really started to change. Timmy became agitated easily and his temper was short. It wasn't unusual for Tim to be angry about something and punch a hole in a wall. Mom often asked what was wrong, to which he would reply, "Nothing." None of us understood what was happening. Tim seemed almost afraid of people and started keeping to himself. Timmy and Jimmy were close. Timmy was the best man in Jim's wedding and the godfather to Jim's son, two jobs he took seriously. They went to concerts together and had most of the same friends. On the night Jimmy's son was born, Jimmy sat with Timmy and told him every last detail as Timmy listened, wide-eyed with excitement. It was this closeness that made it easy for Jimmy to recommend Timmy for a job at the beer store he managed.

One night when they were working, some thugs came in to rob the place. They punched Timmy, knocking him over, and stole cigarettes and lottery tickets. That accelerated Timmy's already paranoid behavior. He started sleeping more and was regularly late for work. Tim's behavior was increasingly disturbing to others as well as to us. He was so withdrawn and would not make eye contact with customers or with the family. He started telling outlandish stories that made sense only to him. His friend Bob found Timmy sitting at the park in tears one night. Timmy had been hearing voices in his head and was scared to death. He didn't know what was happening, and he didn't know what to do about it. It was the beginning of a long and painful journey. It was as if Timmy had stopped showing up for life.

Jimmy was faced with one of the hardest decisions of his life as the owner of the beer store started to complain about Tim's behavior. Jimmy was left with no choice but to fire his brother. As Jim described it, it was one of his darkest memories. Jim had been covering for Timmy for quite some time, but Timmy had pretty much checked out of the job, so the act of firing was only the official close. They had been best friends and had done everything together. Whatever was happening to Timmy seemed like hell enough, and then for Jim to have to deliver the bad news must have been a pain worse than hell for Jim.

It appeared demons had taken over Timmy. The only communication he had with others was to tell them preposterous stories. He gave me his ATM card and personal identification number because he was certain that if he used it someone would read his thoughts, learn his PIN, and steal his money. He opened two different bank accounts, using different names for each in an attempt to confuse anyone who read his thoughts. He spent hours walking around the outside of the house, looking for tunnels that he claimed the CIA had dug under it so they could spy on him. He stopped walking through the campus at Lafayette College, just a few blocks from our house, because he was certain the Russians were building nuclear weapons there. He believed if they thought he knew what they were doing, he would be in danger. His obsessions changed from time to time. He soon became convinced that he was involved with the Patty Hearst case, even though he was only eleven years old at that time.[1] Timmy also claimed to have been on tour with the Beatles and that he and John Lennon were close friends. He said they called him "Little John."

For a time, Timmy was obsessed with New York City and often made the two-hour trip in a car that somehow survived his erratic driving and ridiculous speeds. No one really knew what he did there. Often, he disappeared for an entire day and Mom spent hours worrying about him.

The delusions continued to change and expand, and he thought the family was hiding things from him. As money was becoming scarce, Timmy started sneaking up to the attic of the house to look for baseball cards, we guessed so he could sell them. These were cards that our dad had

collected since he was a kid, and we all added our own over time. Timmy thought Dad was hiding cards from him, under the floor boards. When he found what he thought were his cards, he took off one day. No one knew where he was, and this, as always, made Mom nervous.

---

1. Patty Hearst was the granddaughter of a well-known publishing icon. She became famous in the early '70s when she was abducted from Berkley by a terrorist group who were believed to have beaten and brainwashed her. After being held captive, she became sympathetic to their cause and was soon engaging in their illegal activities. She was arrested and prosecuted. She was found guilty of bank robbery and sentenced to prison.

Finally, Mom received a call from the Pennsylvania state police. Timmy was walking along Route 22 and was picked up because it was unsafe and probably illegal to be walking along a highway. He had been trying to get to Bethlehem, a city about fifteen miles away, to sell the cards. Dad went to get him and brought him home with no understanding of what was happening to Tim.

Timmy stayed in our parent's back room—some might call it a den—instead of his bedroom. He only came out to eat, late at night after everyone had gone to bed. He rarely bathed; he looked like a homeless person. This went on for about six years. It was absolutely heartbreaking. We didn't have computers or the internet to even attempt to look up what could possibly be happening. Timmy was about twenty-nine at this point, and we couldn't force him to do anything. We had no idea what was going on with him and were all afraid for his well-being. It seemed there was no reasoning with him. Our dad, who hated confrontation, told Timmy that something had to change or he would be living at a local homeless shelter, to which Timmy answered, "I've already been there, and it doesn't scare me."

When I was twenty-one, I married and at twenty-five, I had my son, Sean. I lived about twelve miles from my mom but visited almost every day, especially after my son was born. It was about this time when I decided to start seeking help for my brother.

Chapter V
Diagnosis

"And why worry about a speck in your friend's eye when you have a log in yours?"
~Matthew 7:3~

These were the words Timmy spoke to Mom when she suggested help: "And why worry about a speck in your friend's eye when you have a log in yours?" he said. "I am just fine, it's the rest of you with the problem." I've heard it said that if you are mentally unstable, you are usually the last to know.

Just before my son's first birthday, the family had decided that Timmy could no longer go on this way and that my parents surely deserved some peace. I made several phone calls to crisis intervention, psychiatrists, and people I knew in drug recovery programs because I believed that was the root of his problems. I was desperate for some way to help my brother. After a long conversation with an acquaintance who was a recovering alcoholic and a psychotherapist, we decided that an intervention of sorts would be our best course of action. We suspected Tim's problem was no longer being fueled by drugs or alcohol because he had no job and no money, but we suspected that drugs may have triggered what was happening. We had to band together to get him the help he so desperately needed. My other brothers and I got together to plan the intervention. We saw to it that our mom and dad were not in

46

the house, as it would likely be too difficult for them to have to see. I stayed home with my son while the rest of the family gathered at my parents' house. The psychotherapist I had spoken with said to listen for key words that may in some way threaten Tim's life or anyone else: words like "kill" or "suicide." If we heard those words, we were to call the police and tell them that Tim needed to be taken to the hospital for a psychiatric evaluation. Mark had the police phone number on redial, and the intervention began.

None of us can keep from crying when we look back on that day. We knew Timmy needed help, but he seemed so innocent and vulnerable. My brothers ended up ordering Timmy into the dining room. In his fight-or-flight position, he went directly to fight. He believed there was a conspiracy and that his brothers were out to get him. In a mad panic, Timmy tried to take on all the brothers. He swung at everyone, finally connecting with Mark. The voices in his head must have been truly evil for him to have hit anyone. When he finally spoke, they were the words everyone was waiting for, "Someone is going to die here tonight, either me or one of you." That was Mark's cue to go upstairs and hit redial. He explained to the police that we were dealing with someone we believed was mentally ill and that he needed to be taken to the hospital. They held Tim down on the floor until the police arrived. Jimmy stood back, and when the police arrived, he pleaded with them to be gentle. He said the responding officer was a "credit to his profession" and was very gentle with Timmy who had voluntarily placed his hands behind his back and waited to be handcuffed. To this day, that very thought crushes me. The Timmy we all knew and loved would never hurt anyone. He was a gentle and kind soul, always.

Timmy was taken to the nearest hospital, where he was kept in the emergency room because the hospital did not have a psychiatric unit. The following day the hospital held what is known as a 302 hearing, which determines whether a person can be held involuntarily for psychiatric treatment. Timmy was provided an attorney who represented him and his well-being. The hearing involved doctors, a judge, Timmy's lawyer, and all the brothers who were at the intervention the night before. As if the events prior were not heartbreaking enough, now they had to sit with Timmy before a judge and declare him incompetent to make a life-changing decision on his own. It was necessary for the judge to hear from the witnesses that Timmy made a threat to either himself or another. Without asking outright, the judge was leading the questions in a way. Finally, Mark said, "Yes, he said that someone would die here tonight." That was the end of the hearing. Timmy was then transferred to a nearby hospital with a psychiatric unit. We were fortunate to have him so close to home. Often, psychiatric patients are sent to hospitals that have an empty bed, and those are typically far away. Having Timmy at a hospital so close guaranteed that we would be a big part of his treatment.

After many brain scans and conversations with the psychiatrist, Timmy was diagnosed with paranoid schizophrenia, a mental illness in which the patient has audible hallucinations and becomes suspicious and distrustful of others, believing people are reading their thoughts and trying to harm them.[2] He heard two male voices in his head and they were brutal. They mocked him constantly, telling him he was worthless, telling him not to bother to bathe because he was ugly. He told Jim it was like a horror movie being played twenty-four hours a day, seven days a week, in his head. Those voices never allowed him to ask for or accept help. He was a prisoner to his own mind.

We thought this was his first diagnosis; however, while Timmy was in the hospital and we were setting up his bedroom for his return home, we found antipsychotic drugs that he had been prescribed years earlier. He never told us anything, but, clearly, he had sought help at the onset of his illness. This time, he was prescribed Prolixin, a first-generation antipsychotic medication used to treat the symptoms of schizophrenia.[3] Along with the Prolixin, Timmy was prescribed Artane, a medication used for Parkinson's patients that also combats the negative side effects of Prolixin.

I spent many sleepless nights worried about Timmy in that place. He was being seen and treated by a doctor, but the daily disturbances on the ward were the making of nightmares. Timmy had never been away from home before, and his first time was in a place where people were yelling and fighting all day and night.

---

2. "Schizophrenia is a chronic and severe mental disorder that affects how a person thinks, feels, and behaves. People with schizophrenia may seem like they have lost touch with reality. Although schizophrenia is not as common as other mental disorders, the symptoms can be very disabling." (The National Institute of Mental Illness).
3. Prolixin "rebalances dopamine to improve thinking, mood, and behavior" (National Alliance on Mental Illness).

One night when I was leaving, a man was yelling "Why did you save my useless life? I could have fucking died and been done with it, but you saved me for what, to bring me here so I could sit in a mental hospital and be treated like a prisoner?" Another man was strapped to a chair so a nurse could shave his face. None of the patients could have any sharp objects, cords, strings, or anything else they could possibly use to hurt themselves.

Timmy was a model patient. He did everything just as he was asked and was always agreeable. He was scared but happy to have some semblance of his life back, and he wanted to cooperate so that he could go home. Timmy may have been among some violent psychiatric patients, but he was finally getting the help he needed. He had a psychiatrist and was being medicated for the psychosis.

Although Timmy seemed to be in reasonably good spirits, his section of the hospital was the most depressing place I can remember, and I'm glad he had our visits to look forward to. We came every day. We never saw any other visitors—it was as if the other patients had been dropped off there and forgotten. Every afternoon, I strapped my son, Sean, into his car seat, picked up my parents, and drove all of us to the hospital. We took turns going up to visit Timmy because my son was too young to go in. Kids under twelve years old were forbidden to visit the psychiatric floor. One of us stayed in the parking lot walking Sean in his stroller while the others went in, and then we switched. A woman who was a patient looked longingly out the window at my son and asked me if he was my child. The nurse instructed me not to answer any of her questions regarding children. Timmy also stared out the window at Sean.

He was so remorseful for all the time he had lost. He apologized every day for not being there when my son was born. We cried a lot. Imagine losing six years of your life with two abusive voices controlling your every thought. But, he was finally getting help and another opportunity at life. Timmy told Mom of his dream to find someone, fall in love, and perhaps one day marry and have kids. He started to dream of a full life again and it was good.

Timmy stayed in the hospital for about a month, which is nothing compared to the six years he lost prior to his diagnosis, sitting in solitude at our parents' house. During his stay, we brought him cigarettes and any kind of food he wanted. I brought chocolate covered strawberries. While Timmy worked at the beer store, he had become friends with the cashier who later bought a small candy shop in town. She kept all the original recipes from 1931, the year the store had opened. It was a treasure! Every year around Valentine's Day, the store featured chocolate covered strawberries, and they had become a favorite of Tim's. Nothing was too much, and it felt good to bring him things that made him smile.

After a few weeks in the hospital, Tim was afforded passes on the weekends so he could come home for a few hours at a time—with instructions for us to keep an eye open for any unusual behavior. Timmy was so happy for the visits home and there was a light in his eyes again.

Once Timmy was released from the hospital, he continued with outpatient therapy daily. Monday through Friday, he reported to the group and learned skills he had lost over his time of psychosis. He was taught tools to help in the event that the voices came back or he felt out of balance. The family was included in a session or two as we all needed guidance. We were learning warnings signs to know when Tim may be in need of a medicine change. Tim was on a heavy-duty antipsychotic drug and another drug to combat the negative effects of that drug. I drove him each day to outpatient therapy. After therapy, we would go on adventures to lunch, the mall, or anything else he wanted to do. To see the life back in his eyes and the smile on his face was magical to me, and I was grateful beyond words.

I picked Timmy up one afternoon and decided to take him to a music festival in town. My son had brought an old princess phone as a toy for the car ride. There were no cell phones yet, only car phones. As we sat in traffic, I picked up the phone and pretended to make calls. I moved my mouth and motioned my hands as if I was having an intense conversation. The delight I felt when I heard giggling coming from the passenger seat! It was the first time in years that I heard Tim laugh out loud. It was genuine laughter like that of a child, so authentic and pure. His laughter was contagious, and we were both doubled over, relishing the moment.

After about a month, Timmy had finally graduated from outpatient care and was going on monthly visits with a doctor who worked for the county and was closer to home. Tim would go in, speak with the doctor, and receive an injection of his medication that was time released to last for a month. At the end of each month, Tim's behavior would start to change. He noticed it, too, and would even giggle and admit it was time for his meds. Over all, life was finally starting to resemble normal again. Steve, who had seemed lost to Tim, especially after the night of the confrontation, felt closer than ever to him. They spent many nights at a local diner having a midnight breakfast.

Having missed six years of his life, Timmy had some financial hardship. With our dad's help, he applied for Social Security Disability. His initial claim was denied, as I understand is the norm. We took things to the next step and hired an attorney who came highly recommended because he specialized in such cases. Timmy wasn't looking to collect disability from that point forward, only to recover the six years that had been lost. With the attorney's help, Timmy was awarded Social Security Disability benefits on a retroactive basis that made up for his lost time. It was such a relief to have a lump sum of money. He made quick work of finding jobs through a temporary service until an insurance company only a mile from home hired him as a permanent, full-time employee. Now the goal was to buy a car.

Timmy had a few clunkers to hold him over until he could afford a decent car. Because he was so soft-spoken and shy, mechanics found it easy to take advantage of him and did unnecessary work to make an extra buck at Tim's expense. The guy who regularly worked on his car often kept it for extended periods of time. One day, I called the guy, explained that, unlike Timmy, I was aware of his reputation and that I trusted him no further than I could throw him. I explained that for him to be paid, Tim needed the car to go to work and that, if he had any conscience, he would do only what was necessary and return the car at once. The car was done the next day and we never brought it there again. I might be the only girl in the family, but my brothers taught me well. I had a short fuse and a temper to follow. I had a reputation of my own as a sharp-tongued wiseass, and I wasn't afraid to tell someone off if I saw fit. My mom once said, "When you go after someone, they have been thoroughly gone after." Meaning, I had an acid tongue and would dig deep to find words that would unmistakably be taken seriously. Nobody was going to hurt Timmy if I had anything to say about it. So, when it came time for him to buy a new car, I insisted on going with him. I was not about to let some fast-talking, used car salesman take advantage of him.

Timmy wanted a stick shift car. I'll never know why, but it really didn't matter. We went to the Saturn dealership where we found the perfect car. It was a sporty little five-speed and it was just right. Timmy whipped out his checkbook and, without any thought, cut a check for $10,000. I had to drive the car home, and what followed were some painful but laugh-filled driving lessons—another time when laughter filled the car and my heart.

Cars were an interesting part of Tim's story. They had once been a source of humor. John tells the story of a car Timmy once had that he bought from my dad's friend. It was huge and Timmy's driving it was in itself funny. An electrical issue caused the horn to beep every time Timmy made a left-hand turn. Timmy was on his way home from work one night when the entire neighborhood could hear his horn blowing from several blocks away. John was nearly in tears with laughter as Timmy parked the car in front of the house. Once parked, Timmy emerged saying, "Do you know of any weddings in the area?" That was old school Timothy: rather than get upset, turn it into a joke. Sadly, it didn't last as car troubles soon predicted his level of stress and anxiety.

Several months had passed with Timmy going to his monthly appointments when the doctor did the unthinkable. He decided that Timmy should be responsible for his own medication and wrote a prescription. I'm no doctor, but I know that no psychiatrist worth his degree would ever allow a schizophrenic to medicate himself. Timmy did not keep up with his medication. Mom stayed awake late every night, waiting for Timmy to come home from work so she could watch him take his medicine and then go to bed. He grew more and more resistant and finally stopped taking his meds. Mom and I were in a panic, fearing Tim would lose all that he had worked so hard to obtain. I made numerous phone calls to his nurse and doctor, pleading with them to continue the injections, but to no avail. The system failed Timmy.

Chapter VI

The Return of the Demons

I am terrified by this dark thing that sleeps inside me.
~Sylvia Plath, *Elm*~

Looking at Timmy you could see the light dimming in his eyes. The voices were back, and he was becoming more distant. He did, however, continue to work. Timmy was somehow able to function despite what horror was happening in his head. Timmy started to increase his use of cigarettes and alcohol, and his participation in our world was minimal. We all slowly accepted that this was his new normal. Timmy's life became a series of habits. He got up in the morning and had coffee like the rest of us and then spent about two and a half hours in the bathroom getting ready for work. He was fastidious when getting ready to leave the house for any reason, so we only imagined what this entailed. After work, Timmy always walked the six blocks to Wawa for cigarettes and snacks. Once he was home, he drank until he fell asleep. That was his every day. I've heard that alcohol can help quiet the voices in a schizophrenic mind, but recent studies show that this is not accurate.

Just before my son's second birthday, the two of us moved into the house next door to my parents' as I started divorce proceedings. It was a great neighborhood when I was a kid, and I thought the same would be true for my son. I was also guaranteed free babysitting by my mom so I could work. Being next door sure had its benefits.

On a beautiful Saturday in May, the time of year when graduation parties are popping up all over, our neighbors across the street threw a party for their son, and we were all invited. We had a great time and even looked the other way when we saw the underage kids drinking alcohol. That night, Timmy came home from work and began following his normal routine; however, this time was different. When my phone rang at one o'clock in the morning, I could barely understand my mom's frantic voice. I immediately ran next door to find Timmy standing on the porch, covered in blood. He was almost unrecognizable as blood covered his entire face. I asked who had done this and he pointed across the street and said, "They did." What was a routine trip to Wawa turned into what I can only imagine to be a horror. Three of the kids from the party across the street had gone adventuring and found themselves playing hockey in an open grass field that happened to be along Tim's path home from the store. It's important to remember here that Timmy was so quiet and soft-spoken that he would never even make eye contact with anyone. He spoke to no one and always minded his own business. When the kids saw Timmy coming, they approached him and, we're a little unclear what happened next, but it ended with them beating Timmy over the head with a hockey stick until the stick broke in half. At that point, they all ran, leaving Timmy on the sidewalk, bleeding.

Timmy made his way home, quite shaken, and had Mom call the police. When the police arrived, we explained that the kids had been drinking all night and many of them were underage. When the officer went across the street, it seems he found one of his fellow officers' sons at the party and from that point forward, very few questions were asked. I asked if an ambulance was coming to take Timmy to the hospital, to which he replied, "No, you can take him." It was clear he was brushing us off. I took Timmy to the emergency room, where he was given fifteen stitches in his head. When we left the hospital, it was now five o'clock in the morning, and we drove to where the attack happened. There we found Timmy's glasses, his bag from Wawa, and the hockey stick. It was clear the police had not come here, and no investigation was even happening.

The next morning, Dennis went across the street with a notebook and pen, knocked on the door, and demanded the neighbor give him the names of those who did this. If the police weren't going to help us, then we were going to take matters into our own hands. I hate that he was a target for spoiled kids with an automatic "get-out-of-jail-free card" because they had connections in the police department. The woman immediately took a defensive attitude and refused to speak with any of us. After she threatened to call the police, Dennis stood back saying, "Please do. I'll wait." The police came again, and I handed them the hockey stick and Wawa bag covered in blood. We promised we were not going away and that if we had to involve lawyers and such, we were prepared to see this through until someone was punished.

Within a week, an investigator came to the house and showed Timmy a yearbook, and Tim was able to identify all three boys. Tim already struggled with trust and was now faced with three assailants whom he would have to confront in court. Once all three were notified, the court hearing was scheduled. They were expected to plead guilty, but we would still have to face them at the hearing. With increasing paranoia, Timmy was refusing to go to the trial. He didn't want to face these kids again and I can't say I blame him. I was afraid of what I might say, and my mom made me promise to keep my mouth shut. My dad, who raised his voice about three times in his life, raised it with Timmy explaining that these kids were not getting away with this and that he must go. Timmy always listened to Dad and so he went. All three kids pleaded guilty and were given fines, basically a slap on the wrist. They went on to college and had successful lives while Timmy never recovered from that night and never walked to Wawa again.

Slowly, all Timmy's eccentricities returned; however, it was different this time. He was much more docile and he had no temper, like the old Timmy. The paranoia had shifted to new areas of his life. Timmy loved expensive sneakers and would regularly update his collection, although I'm pretty sure he never intended to have a collection. He would buy a pair, and if he happened to step too close to dog poop, he would never wear them again. He would kick them off outside the door and leave them there until someone else moved them.

He shopped regularly at a shop in town that made custom suits and sold expensive, high-class clothing. Timmy had no place to wear these clothes, but he had a closet full of them. When he hadn't been to the store in a while, they would call the house checking on their most valued customer. Before long, those phone calls were looking for past due payments as Timmy's paranoia had now manifested in a fear of opening mail. Bills piled up and sat, ignored. Tim opened two types of mail, his paycheck (as he was the only employee left who did not have direct deposit) and his car insurance bill. Tim seemed to recognize that driving was a privilege, and he took all matters related to his car seriously.

In preparation for a house inspection to allow Mom do a reverse mortgage, Tim was asked to clean his room. He was beyond what you would call a pack rat. Clothing, sneakers, money, papers, shower supplies lined the floor and made it nearly impossible to even walk in there. Timmy told us to go ahead and clean. He wanted nothing to do with it. As we cleaned, the most alarming thing we found was close to a hundred empty boxes of lice shampoo. Tim had asked our mom once to check if he had lice. Of course, he didn't have it, but the paranoia was overwhelming, and he regularly used this as a preventative method because his illness convinced him to do so. There was no reasoning. Most of the clothes he purchased from the shop I mentioned sat with the tags still on; he never opened them. We also had to clean the patio out behind the house because Timmy had been putting cigarettes out in the cracks between the stones that made up the wall. There were so many that the wall almost looked like it was held together by cigarette butts.

Chapter VII
A Beautiful Soul

Out of suffering have emerged the strongest souls; the most massive characters are seared with scars.
~Khalil Gibran, *The Broken Wings*~

Timmy had such a softness about him. He had the most gorgeous blue eyes, but they were filled with pain and emptiness. He was clearly so far away. He was kind to every person and critter he ever met. I had a Chihuahua named Angus that I adopted from a shelter. Angus came from a rough life. He had been abused and was left emaciated with a telephone cord around his neck. He was taken to the ASPCA and deemed unfit for adoption because they thought he would not survive. My son and I took him home as a foster, and he ended up thriving. Angus wasn't a big fan of most people, but he loved Timmy and Timmy clearly loved him. Tim would lean over and very gently, with the back of his hand, pet Angus on the head. He always spoke to him in a whisper. Angus would run to Timmy any time we visited. Perhaps they recognized each other's suffering and found comfort in that understanding.

Most schizophrenics are described as having a lack of empathy. There were many times Timmy seemed to fit this description, but then he would do something surprising to all of us and show deep concern.

My son and I had been out one night when a thunderstorm erupted. Angus was always afraid of storms and was home alone that night. The next morning when I saw Timmy, he said, "I hope you don't mind that I went into your house with mom's spare key. We were having a thunderstorm and I know Angus is afraid, so I went in to sit with him so he would feel safe." This is typical of Timmy. Regardless of voices and stereotypes, Timmy couldn't help but be his true self.

The news is often guilty of feeding the incorrect stereotype of mental illness by sensationalizing stories and making sure it's known that a particular criminal "suffered from schizophrenia."[4] This has always bothered me because I know firsthand that most schizophrenics are of no harm to anyone. Timmy would sooner die than hurt anyone. His illness may have clouded his emotions, but it never erased them. Timmy always cared for others, and I cannot remember a time when he said no to a favor Mom or I would ask. After our father passed away in 2001, Timmy made sure our mom was cared for. He did all of her food shopping, took her to appointments, did all of her banking, and treated her with the utmost kindness. Nothing was too much to ask of him. Except to take his medicine.

Timmy was a marvel. We knew he wasn't using his medication, yet he worked every day, paid his car insurance, maintained his car, and lived what was for him a normal life. That is unheard of for someone with an untreated mental illness. He had great taste in clothing and beer. He loved the classic BBC programs and watched them often with Mom. He

---

4. "Most people with schizophrenia are not violent. In fact, most violent crimes are not committed by people with schizophrenia" (National Institute of Mental Health).

loved shopping for fine crystal and jewelry and had a sophisticated sense of humor. I remember going to look for a Christmas tree in my ex-husband's pickup truck. I was driving, Mom sat in the middle, and Tim was in the passenger seat. We had gotten lost and our patience was quickly fading. The more lost we got, the ruder other drivers seemed, and we were all about done with the holidays when Tim blurted out, "Merry fucking Christmas." I had to pull over because all three of us laughed so hard that we couldn't see straight.

On April 12, 2003, we were celebrating my son's tenth birthday, which was actually on the eighth, but we had his party on the following Saturday. It was the first warm Spring day in Pennsylvania and we had two parties planned—the early one was for the kids and the later was for the adults. My son had the time of his life. After the party had ended, my mom sat down to rest for a few minutes and I went next door letting Mom know I'd be back to clean up in a bit. I was only home for a few minutes when there was frantic banging on my front door and my mom yelling my name. She was holding out the phone to me saying, "It's Stella (Mark's mother-in-law). She wanted to know if someone was with me." I took the phone away, and Stella explained that there had been an accident and that Mark was killed. My mom and I both collapsed on the steps. Sean, who had just had the best day was watching us crumble. I told him to go get Uncle Steve. We started making phone calls for the family to come back to the house. We called the insurance company where Timmy worked and told him what had happened. He hung up the phone but didn't come home. John and Steve drove to his work and told the security guard what had happened and that they wanted Timmy to come home. Timmy acknowledged the information and, in a mechanical way, went back to his work. Timmy's supervisor insisted that Tim go home and he did. How horrible this disease was to not allow Timmy to feel the loss of his brother! It had only been eighteen months since our father had died, and Timmy was numb. He never appeared to process things like the rest of us; he seemed almost catatonic.

As much as all of us worried about Timmy, Mark worried the most. Being the oldest, he felt responsible for all of us. After Mark married, he and his wife moved to Arizona and then to San Diego, CA. It was a beautiful spring day in the high desert, and Mark was riding his motorcycle. Mark often took day trips by himself and, on this day, rode up into the high desert of California. On the road that same day was a family admiring the spring flowers off to the side of the road. The driver of the car was drifting off the road when he pulled the wheel suddenly, and his vehicle went over the yellow line and hit Mark head on. The driver tried to administer CPR, but it was too late. It was heartbreaking. But, at least Mark died doing what he loved, and I like to think he was smiling at the majesty of the scenery.

Mark used to call often to speak with Mom and she told him tales of happiness so he wouldn't worry. Once he hung up, he would call me next door and say, "I just spoke to Mom, so maybe you can tell me how things really are." I would fill him in on the latest regarding our dad, tell him how our mom was and fill in any blanks left by Mom. His second question, without fail, was always, "How's Timothy?" I did my best to answer that question because none of us really knew how Timmy was doing. For all the years since Mark died, that question has haunted me.

It soon became my own question each time I called my mom. Her answer depended on whether Timmy was there or at work. She never spoke about him while he was home. She was afraid to ever offend him and damage the trust he had in her. He trusted so few people and she wanted to remain one of them.

As time went on, Timmy trusted fewer people. It seemed to stem from the night of the initial intervention. He stopped trusting anyone who was there that night. Mom and I had not been there, and he seemed to view us as his allies. As I mentioned, Timmy took care of our mom, making sure she always had candy for when her sugar would drop, running errands to the store and to pick up wine, and making trips to the bank to cash checks for her. These were things he did without having been asked; he just knew, and he cared. He and our mom had a bond. They needed each other. Mom, then in her mid-eighties and struggling with many health issues of her own, including type 2 diabetes, made sure that whatever food Timmy wanted for dinner was made. He shopped and she cooked. On nights he had off from work, he bought prepared seafood as a treat for both of them. Despite the schizophrenia, Timmy had a depth about him. He was driven by kindness and thoughtfulness, which is something so foreign to someone with a severe mental illness. I have always and will always describe Timmy as a pure and beautiful soul.

Among other things, Timmy was always good for a short-term loan. I have always been horrible with money, no secret there. Anytime I ever needed anything, Timmy was there with his checkbook ready. He never accepted repayment. He once loaned me $2000 towards a car. I had my online banking set up to send him a check every two weeks. After a few months, I started getting notices from the bank that the money was being redeposited because Timmy never cashed any of the checks. Mom said he never even opened any of the envelopes, even after I told him what they were.

With my mom getting older and my no longer living next door, Jimmy and his wife Charlene started hosting Thanksgiving. Sadly, Timmy would not go anywhere for any holiday. It was heartbreaking knowing that on those holidays Timmy was home alone. I will never know whether he felt hurt, abandoned, or just nothing. A plate was always made up to take home to him. He sat quietly in the back room, looking at a blank TV screen, and ate his Thanksgiving dinner alone. This would be the extent of holidays for Tim as he stopped participating in family events. Thanksgivings and Christmases passed like the ticking of a clock until Thanksgiving of 2014. Timmy was now fifty years old and, again, spending this day home alone. This day, life changed for all of us.

In the previous months, Timmy had been struggling with dental problems. His speech was beginning to sound garbled, but he insisted he was fine and having dental work done. That night, while the rest of us were enjoying dinner at Jimmy and Charlene's house, Timmy took himself to the emergency room. We were devastated that he did this without letting us know. None of us could be there for him. I spoke to him the following day, and he said that it was an infection in his tooth. Steve saw the paperwork from the hospital. The diagnosis of angioedema made absolutely no sense to him when looking at Tim's symptoms, which seemed only to affect his tooth.[5] Timmy was told to follow up with an ear, nose, and throat specialist within two days. He made an appointment, and we all waited on pins and needles, trying to get a straight answer from him. The fact that Tim was suffering enough to have gone to the hospital meant a great deal. Tim didn't trust doctors but was desperate to seek one. We all knew this was serious yet were unable to help him, and none of us was sure what to believe as he often spoke in delusional ways.

The day of the appointment, I must have called twenty times to see if he had left the house, and each time Mom sadly answered, "No." Tim never did go to that appointment. My mom had received a few phone calls confirming appointments with a dentist, and on the day of one of Tim's appointments, we had a pretty significant snow storm. Tim left the house, and my mom called me several hours later, crying, to tell me that Tim hadn't come home yet and she was worried sick. John drove to the dental office, where they were unable to give him any information, and I called several times with the same response. My final phone call ended when the receptionist said, "He left a few hours ago."

Timmy's speech was getting worse and less understandable. There was clearly something seriously wrong, but Timmy refused to deal with things in a reasonable manner because of his mental illness. Every time I visited Mom, I asked Tim if he wanted to go to the doctor, and I told

5. "Angioedema: an acute or chronic disorder that effects the mucous membranes and deepest layers of the skin along with underlying tissue and that is marked by rapid swelling, large welts, and pain." Merriam-Webster Dictionary

him I would gladly go with him. He would acknowledge my offer and then walk away.

Soon, he looked like a shadow of himself. He had lost quite a bit of weight and his steps were so delicate, as if he were tippy-toeing. Each time I saw him, he was holding the side of his face. He came home from work one night, leaned in towards our mom, and gently said, "I think I may want to quit my job." Without knowing what was going on, Mom pleaded with him not to do that. She told him he would lose his benefits. Timmy never brought it up again, and he continued to work, every day, never calling in sick. Not one to complain, he never let on that anything was wrong.

On December 22, Timmy went Christmas shopping and came back with beautifully wrapped gifts. It just so happened that day was our mom's birthday. He walked over to where she was sitting, leaned over, handed her a box, and said softly, "Happy birthday, Mom." What this must have felt like to our mom is something we'll never really understand: to see her son, so frail and so sick, be so selfless, just as he had always been. I don't know the heartache she felt when Mark died, and now she had so many sleepless nights, worrying about Timmy. To say she is a tough lady is simply an understatement.

It had now been five months and Timmy was clearly not getting better. In fact, he was looking critical. It was nearly impossible to understand his speech, and he walked around clutching the side of his face. After a few failed attempts to get together with the brothers due to snowstorms, we finally settled on Sunday, May 17, at Jimmy's house to discuss Tim and what we could possibly do to help him. It had been nearly six months since Timmy's trip to the emergency room, and it was evident we needed to step in. Steve said that a few days earlier, he had noticed a lump on Tim's neck. This made things seem even more urgent. During that meeting, I called my ex-sister-in-law, Donna, who is involved with National Alliance on Mental Illness (NAMI) because her son suffers from schizoaffective disorder.[6] She advised me to call crisis intervention to see if they could take Timmy to the hospital or advise us what to do. Typically, they respond when someone is suicidal, but we had hopes that his lack of care for himself would be enough to go on. Donna and I had many conversations about schizophrenia. She taught a class to families of the mentally ill. In one of her lessons, she attempts to simulate what goes on in a schizophrenic's head. To make her point, she asks one person to sit at a table and try to write a thought while several others gather around them, speaking all at the same time. She says that is a normal day to a schizophrenic, which makes it that much more remarkable that Timmy had held his job for twenty years.

After my conversation with Donna, my brothers and I decided to take action. John, Sean, Dennis, and I went to our mom's house immediately. We hoped it would be cut and dried, but I think we all knew better. Mom was outraged when she found out that we were planning to confront Timmy in another intervention and demand he go to the hospital for help. She thought for sure this would ruin Timmy's trust in the two of us and would, as she said, "end disastrously." I

---

6. "Schizoaffective disorder is a mental disorder in which a person experiences a combination of schizophrenia symptoms, such as hallucinations or delusions, and mood disorder symptoms, such as depression or mania." Mayo Clinic

pleaded with her through tears, telling her that he was suffering and that, as the people who loved him as much as we did, we had to help him. I told her that she would never forgive herself if she looked the other way and then found him dead one day. She insisted we leave well enough alone because once I blew the trust he had in me, his survival would mean a lonely life of trusting no one. I told her that as long as there was breath in my lungs, I would do everything possible to help him. Since Jimmy and Charlene had gone through the very first intervention years ago, it was decided they should take Mom and return to their house.

After Mom had gone, John, Dennis, Sean, and I were left. I went out back to the patio, where Timmy was having a cigarette. I saw that he was clutching the side of his neck, and I asked him to please let me see. When Timmy lifted his hand, what I saw knocked the breath out of me. Timmy had a growth the size of an orange on the side of his neck. It was evident that he was in quite a bit of pain. I pleaded with him, "Timmy, please let me take you to the hospital. You need to be seen by a doctor." He shrugged his shoulders, as he usually did, said no, and went into the house. I went back to the front porch to tell the others what had happened. I told them that Timmy was in serious danger and that we had to do whatever was necessary to get him to the hospital. I called crisis intervention but was told that unless it was a suicide threat or threat against someone's life, they were unable to help. We felt totally helpless. I had been told that lack of self care is reason to have someone taken to the hospital without their consent, and now they were saying there was nothing they could do.

It was clear we had to do this with no help, so my brothers and I decided that together we would just go up to Timmy's room and confront him and that we would not take no for an answer. When we got to the top of the steps, I opened Timmy's bedroom door to find him in bed with the blankets over his head. I said, "Timmy, we are all out here. We love you so much and we are concerned about you. There is no reason for you to be in this much pain; I can get you help. Please let me take you to the hospital. I promise, I will be your voice. Anything that they do will have to pass by me first." Much to all our surprise, Timmy lowered the blanket, lifted his head and said, "Okay."

In typical Timmy fashion, it took a very long time for him to get ready to go. We started to believe that had he agreed to go just so we would leave him alone. I wasn't going anywhere, and neither were the others. We were prepared to stay there all night if necessary. I gave him a few more minutes and then went to check on him. He was out back having one last cigarette, knowing that once we got to the hospital, it would be a while before his next. He was so weak that it took quite some time for him to get to my car. He was very proud and would not allow anyone to help him. Once we were in the car, I reiterated that I would be his voice. I promised him that I would not leave him during any of this. I asked him if it would be okay for the doctors to discuss his care with me, he obliged, and I told him he may have to sign papers to give them that permission. He looked at me and, in his garbled voice, said, "You handle this." A sense of relief rushed over me. We were finally getting him help.

Chapter VIII
Diagnosis Number Two

On the way to the hospital, I asked Timmy to make sure he had his insurance cards ready. He said he didn't have any insurance. Here's a guy who works for an insurance company yet has no insurance. I assured him it would be all right; I didn't want him to have anything more to worry about. God knows, this was more than enough.

After we got through triage, I sent Tim out to the waiting room while I went back in to explain to the nurse that he had schizophrenia and would never admit it and that his account of what was happening may be skewed. She put it in her notes but suggested I tell the emergency room doctor as well. They finally called us back. It had been a long wait, but we were all there: Dennis, Jimmy, Steve, John, and I.

The emergency room doctor was shocked by what he saw on Tim's neck. He was just as shocked to see that Tim, who was 6'1", weighed 118 pounds. He pulled some fluid out of the cyst with a syringe and had Tim go for a CT scan. We were bracing ourselves for the worst. I started questioning why this would happen to him—the sweetest person I know, and he was in so much pain! Every one of us would have gladly stepped in to take the pain so that he wouldn't have to suffer. He, of all people, surely did not deserve this, whatever it was.

The doctor came back and put us all at ease by telling us it was a severe infection. He said he had called an ear, nose, and throat specialist, who would have to do surgery right away, and that Timmy would be fine. We all breathed for the first time that day. I went outside to call Mom who was frantically waiting at home for any news. We could almost hear the rosary beads clicking together as she begged God and all the angels and saints to spare Timmy any additional suffering. He had had enough, for God's sake. She was relieved to hear that there was a fix in place. Tim took very seriously our agreement to let me handle things, right down to the doctor asking him how he felt. He would look to me to answer or give him a nod that let him know it was okay for him to answer. Speaking was very difficult and painful, so I answered most of the questions. Any paperwork that came to his room he instructed the nurse to give to me. I felt honored to be trusted with such important responsibilities.

Since none of us knew just how much alcohol Timmy drank, we wanted to be sure to cover that base. He said he hadn't been drinking, but I advised the doctor that he had been using alcohol to fall asleep and there may be a risk of withdrawal. He ordered Ativan to keep his nerves calm in case withdrawal were to set in.

One of the nurses, who happened to be a family friend, asked how we got bumped to the top shelf regarding the ear, nose, and throat specialist. He said Dr. Yen was the cream of the crop and to get him on a Sunday night was especially rare. He told us you couldn't even call his office and get an appointment with him because he was always booked solid. With a reference like that, how could you not feel at ease? Dennis and I were in the room with Timmy when Dr. Yen came in. This guy was a pistol! The level of energy, and at that hour, was intense. We were expecting to hear details of the procedure to be performed that night and get things rolling. What we got was like a punch in the gut.

After the introductions, he went right to business. He went on to tell us that this was not an infection as we had been told. He believed it to be a rather extensive and well-established squamous cell carcinoma. In other words, Timmy had cancer. Dr. Yen felt it had spread throughout most of Tim's jaw, tongue, throat, and perhaps even further, but knowing the extend would require more testing. He believed Tim was in stage four. We were bowled over. Dennis fell back in the chair and I was speechless as I stood alongside the bed. Tim sat, nodding his head, but clearly did not comprehend what had just been said. Hell, no one could absorb that kind of information that quickly. We were devastated. I went out to call the brothers who had gone home. Dennis was across the parking lot throwing up, and I could not even form words through my tears. We gathered the brothers together at the hospital to discuss how we would tell Mom. I wanted to wait until the next day and let her get a good night's sleep with the thought that he would have surgery and be fine, but Steve, who lived with her, was certain he couldn't pull off an act like that, knowing he would see her when he got home. It was decided that I would stay with Timmy while the brothers went to tell our mom. I tried to imagine how she would feel at one in the morning, seeing four of her boys come through the door. A mother never gives up hope and she clung to it with everything she had. She had to hold on for herself and for Timmy. She said later she was certain they were there to tell her that Tim had passed away.

The brothers sat down and, as gently as possible, told Mom what had happened. To watch the hope disappear from her eyes must have been overwhelming. She had already buried her oldest and now was facing the reality that her youngest son would likely be taken, too. They say God doesn't give you more than you can handle, and I say that is bullshit. That was way more than any of us could handle, especially Mom.

I stayed with Timmy until he was settled in a room. He was moved from the emergency department to the intensive care unit. I assured him he would be safe there and that I'd be back first thing in the morning. They gave him some pretty potent pain medication and he was already drifting off to sleep when I left. I finally got home around 2:30 a.m. and opened a beer, which I never drank. I was sick to my stomach from the rollercoaster that the day had been and only had a few hours before I promised I would be back.

The next morning, after very little sleep, I grabbed some coffee and got to the hospital, where they said Timmy had already been asking for me. Tim had gotten up at some point during the night and gotten dressed. I thought for sure he was going to make a break for it, but he was cold and tried to put on as many clothes as he could. Timmy was always cold, so this really came as no surprise. He was being well cared for in the ICU. His nurse that day was Katie, a friend of my niece, who is also a Katie. She was awesome. She checked in more often than any other nurse. She made sure Tim was treated with dignity and respect. At some point during that day, each of the brothers as well as Mom and Charlene came to visit. We kept conversation light and even joked about the lovely robe Tim got to wear and the "gourmet" food. We smiled through our internal despair, for Tim's sake. It was later in the day when Dr. Yen came in and wanted to get a biopsy from inside Tim's throat. Imagine your worst sore throat and multiply that by at least one hundred. That is the level of pain Tim was feeling, and now they were going to dig into the tumor for testing. They gave him fentanyl and I held his hand while the doctor took a sample. My heart broke to see a single tear roll down Tim's face. He never complained about being in pain or being sick. In fact, he had worked until 11:00 the night before I had taken him to the hospital. He was already at stage four cancer with a huge tumor that had no more room to grow inside, so it pushed through to the outside of his neck. The cancer had literally eaten through his neck. Every step Tim took was agonizing, yet he never missed a day of work. He had mentioned to Mom, weeks earlier that he wanted to quit his job, but she was worried he would lose his benefits, which it turns out he didn't have. Rather than go against Mom's wishes, he dutifully kept his job and never said another word about it. Mom still cries to think of how he continued to run errands for her. That was Tim: brave, strong, and loyal. The only thing he really wanted was a cigarette, so they pacified him by giving him a nicotine patch, but it wasn't the same.

On Tuesday, Timmy signed over power of attorney to me, both medical and financial. We couldn't predict that Tim would be so cooperative. Getting those documents together was no small feat! Rich, my boyfriend, and I had a friend who was an attorney. Rich reached out to him in desperation to get this resolved since Timmy could check himself out of the hospital at any time or pass away with financial pieces in the air that would take months to settle, and our mom would surely need the funds should he pass away. That friend got the paperwork and emailed it to Rich, saying that as long as there were two unrelated witnesses, Tim and I could sign them and everything would be legally binding. After receiving the documents, Rich found several discrepancies in wording and fixed them. He then emailed our friend to let him know that he had looked into the documents and had changed some of the language that had been erroneously added. Our friend's response floored us.

The email to Rich read:

(Personal communication – May 19, 2015)

What you are missing is good manners and thoughtfulness. I don't know if you mean to be critical, judgmental and insulting as opposed to coming by it naturally. In the end, does it really matter? I'm sure you perceive yourself as simply being direct, forthright and honest. Perhaps you should consider the recipient's perspective.

You texted me yesterday, in your very insistent way, to tell me: "Kate needs help immediately, like today." No inquiry as to whether I was able to handle an emergent request, or as to what other burdens life may have thrown my way yesterday. So…, I drop EVERYTHING and tend to your issues. Time I could ill afford. No…, I'm not an estate lawyer. Never claimed to be. I clearly misread the statute-not the one you referenced but one dealing with shares of others than surviving spouse. If you so adroitly found the correct answer – as well as satisfactory POA form – upon ten minutes of time then that begs the question as to why you did not make such a nominal investment of time to begin with.

That email response to both the email below and the one you sent at 10:25. The "incorrect" reading of the statute notwithstanding, I spent over 3 hours on your urgent request yesterday. THREE HOURS I COULD ILL-AFFORD. No invoice shall be forthcoming. No need to keep me apprised of anything.

Pissed off. Signed.

To say I was shocked would be an understatement. This man was a friend and we loved him. We had been there for him through some of his difficult times and had never asked for reciprocation. We had offered to pay his legal fees for doing this, and he insisted that friends didn't charge for such things. The direct hit to the heart of his saying not to keep him apprised of anything was more that I could bear during such a heartbreaking time.

As Tim became weaker and less able to communicate, he asked that I make sure everything be taken care of: communication with doctors, appointments, medications, and all his care from that point forward. I promised I would. It was a relief because I now knew that he would not check himself out of the hospital or turn away any necessary care, not that I planned to ever be away from his side. My name was on the papers because he trusted me, yet all the decisions would be made by all of us collectively, and thank God for that. No one person could possibly sort through the madness that came next. Tim was visited by several doctors each day. They all painted a rather grim picture as they told us the extent of his cancer. It seemed every morning when I walked in, a new doctor was in the room. Tim was an anomaly and the doctors marveled at his ability to have gone so long without medical treatment. I acquired a pretty extensive collection of business cards between doctors and social workers.

Knowing Tim stood little to no chance of surviving, we scheduled no chemotherapy or radiation, yet the radiology oncologist was pretty insistent on getting a dentist in to discuss tooth extractions. Radiation weakens the bones in the jaw, and osteonecrosis—or breakdown of bone and blood supply to the gums—makes teeth become loose and fall out, causing a choking hazard. Because of this issue, the teeth are extracted prior to radiation treatment. But, we had decided not to seek further treatment, either chemotherapy or radiation, so I was confused by this doctor's determination to pull Tim's teeth.

Timmy had been hearing bits and pieces and still wanted to be involved in the decisions. He wanted to live, and he wanted to fight, or at least he thought so at the time. There was no way in hell I was going to let them extract his teeth when we were told he had a less than 10 percent chance of surviving. The brothers all agreed, and Mom was horrified at the thought. She adamantly insisted that his teeth be left alone. That led to one hell of an argument over the phone between the radiology oncologist and me. An internal medicine intern who saw my need for a hug, regularly, was behind the desk while I was on the phone, that argument. She said afterwards that all my points were valid and that she was proud of me for standing up and doing what was right for my brother.

I was crumbling under the overwhelming weight, but she assured me I was doing just fine. God, it didn't feel like it. I was handed the responsibility of a human life that meant the world to me. I couldn't take his pain anymore. I was pleading and begging God to ease it for him. Thankfully, my brothers were allies. We made all the decisions together. I called Jimmy just after that argument and I fell apart. I was certain I could not handle this. It was after that tense phone call with the radiology oncologist that I asked Dr. Yen, who had been the lead doctor since the emergency room, to step outside and have an off-the-record heart-to-heart. We discussed how the family had decided not to treat the psychiatric piece. The last time Tim was treated for schizophrenia, he spent months feeling remorse for the time he had lost. It would be cruel to bring him back from a psychotic state just to tell him he was dying. Jimmy joined us, and I told Dr. Yen about the earlier argument and that we were desperate for some essence of understanding.

"You are going to hear this from every doctor on the case," said Dr. Yen. "Radiology guys want to do radiation, chemo guys want to do chemotherapy, dentists want to do dental work, and so on. You will have to weed through all of it and do what is in Tim's best interest. In my professional opinion, Tim has less than a 10 percent chance of surviving, but as a doctor, I would surely want to try. As a family member, I would want to make him comfortable and treat things as they come. No one wants to suffocate, and that is ultimately what will happen. That is when

I would see him again and do a tracheostomy." Removing the tumor was impossible. The doctor said they would have had to destroy the structure of half of Tim's head just to get all the cancer. The cancer was too well established, and even radiation would only have about a 1 percent chance of success. We had to decide: start palliative care or move forward with radiation and chemotherapy.[7]

The next morning, I went in to find that Timmy's cyst had ruptured while he was showering. It was a tremendous relief for him as the pressure was almost gone. But now there was a gaping hole in the side of his neck. Since that was from the tumor, it would never heal. They tested its contents to determine that there was no infection; it was just an overgrowth from the tumor.

Tim's ability to eat continued to decrease. He was sent for a video fluoroscopic swallowing exam (VFSE), a test that uses an X-ray to monitor swallowing. While Timmy swallowed different thicknesses and consistencies of food, the doctor would be able to see if any of it was entering his lungs, which could ultimately cause pneumonia. I was invited to go along and watch from a protected room. It was incredibly sad to see Timmy struggle through that test, yet somehow it made me feel even closer to him. I taped some of the procedure with my phone to show the others. It was pretty clear that soon Tim would not be able to swallow anything. He was encouraged to eat what he could but was

---

7. "Palliative care is a specialized medical care for people with serious illnesses. It is appropriate at any age and at any stage in a serious illness and can be provided along with curative treatment. Palliative care focuses on providing patients with relief from the symptoms and the stress of a serious illness. The goal is to improve quality of life for both the patients and the family." (Home Health and Hospice Care)

warned that the thinner liquids, when swallowed, were going into his lungs. Over time, that could result in pneumonia. If Timmy was to undergo any kind of treatment, it was important for him to gain weight, which he couldn't do with his inability to chew and swallow, so the doctor had a feeding tube inserted. While Tim was under anesthesia for that procedure, the ear, nose, and throat doctor took another look down his esophagus to see if there was any other evident cancer. The hospital was new and did not have the equipment to perform a positron emission tomography (PET) scan to show the extent of the cancer throughout the body. That would have to be done as an outpatient procedure after Tim's release. In the meantime, he received calories through a tube that went through his abdomen and directly into his stomach. Knowing that Tim would be sent home with this, along with many instructions, scared the hell out of me. It was a lot!

Rich and I had been preparing to move to Arizona and my packing came to a screeching halt when things unfolded with Timmy. I figured that my part of the move may have to be delayed and I'd meet Rich in Arizona at a later date, but Rich waited so we would make the move together. One day, after having spent every waking moment at the hospital, my friend Wendy texted and insisted she come rescue me from the hospital for a break. She knew better than anyone the need for that: her daughter Averi was diagnosed with leukemia when she was two years old. Wendy spent two months at the hospital and never left her daughter's side. She then spent the next several years regularly driving two hours each way to Philadelphia for chemo and follow-up appointments. She and Averi came to take me to dinner, and Averi brought a handmade get-well card for Timmy. Although Timmy didn't know Averi, he kept that card with him, both in the hospital and after he came home. He seemed to connect with the innocence with which it was made.

For Tim's final night in the hospital, he was moved out of the ICU and onto another floor. I was asked if we wanted to put a do-not-resuscitate (DNR) order in place. The questions just kept getting more and more painful to answer. As a family, we had decided to go to no heroic efforts should something happen, so I signed the papers. Before leaving the hospital, I had meetings with doctors, social workers, dieticians, and therapists. We had to arrange for home care nurses and for delivery of the feeding tube food and all the necessities to the house. I had Timmy help me make a shopping list of everything he thought he could eat or drink.

He came home on Friday, and I told him he was officially retired and would never have to go back to work again. He was pleased with that. Rich reached out to Tim's boss, Kevin, to let him know what was going on. Kevin said they had been worried sick about him. He had tried for months to get Tim to go to the doctor. He was grateful Tim was getting help but heartbroken about the diagnosis. It was only a day or two later that Tim received flowers and a beautiful card from his coworkers. He read that card at least ten times and smiled every time at all the personal notes. We never knew he had such close relationships with anyone. We were told that it was phenomenal that someone with unmedicated schizophrenia could hold a job for almost twenty years. Not only had he held that job, but he was loved there. I'm told he was part of a team and was considered family. Our own family took great joy in knowing that. The rewards in looking past Tim's eccentricities were his qualities as a good friend, coworker, and fantasy football teammate. Kevin, in particular, was crushed. He came by the house one night after I left. I found notes the next morning with the names of all the Beatles, listed in order of importance according to Tim and Kevin. They had a great visit and Tim was happy for it.

Timmy was an avid fisherman, and he loved to head out to fish long before the sun was up. He never kept anything he caught; he must have just liked the sport of it. He loved to be alone and I'm sure he enjoyed the quiet time. He always had his fishing rod, tackle box, and hat in the back of his car. Unable now to speak, Tim communicated by writing notes. We wrote a lot about possibly going fishing one morning. He was on a heavy dose of oxycodone, so no one wanted him to go alone. He kept a close eye on the weather and followed the news about local fishing tournaments. It was so nice to see him get excited about something.

The first weekend home came and went quickly. It was Memorial Day weekend and we had a small cookout in Tim's honor. I did my best to make foods that he could still swallow, but it was becoming more and more difficult. While Timmy was in the hospital, he spoke about two things: a big juicy hamburger with baked beans and chocolate covered strawberries, of course. It's almost as though he remembered my bringing them to him years earlier when he was in the psychiatric unit. Tim's friend, the one who owns the shop in town with all handmade chocolates, found out Tim was asking for them; she made a batch especially for him and delivered them to the house. Sadly, Tim couldn't eat them, but he asked that I make sure the others enjoy them.

The food that Timmy could have came in a can, and we poured about seven cans a day through the feeding tube. Timmy trusted me to do that, but I knew there was a day coming up when I wouldn't be there to do it. I had a colonoscopy scheduled, which became a bit of a joke to Timmy. Here I was, force-feeding him while I was emptying myself. I showed Tim and the other brothers how to do the tube feedings. Tim learned to do it with ease but lacked the motivation to keep it up. Still, I showed him how to crush his medication so he could easily put it through the feeding tube or mix it with pudding and eat it. We wanted to keep him swallowing for as long as possible so he could enjoy the taste of at least some foods.

I arrived one day to find Timmy out back having a cigarette. He had been wearing a nicotine patch given to him in the hospital with instructions to quit smoking. He was trying to hide it from me. I sat with him and explained that he should not wear the nicotine patch and smoke at the same time but if he wanted to smoke he could. At that point, I wasn't going to take anything he enjoyed away from him.

The next week was filled with appointments, and he finally got the PET scan. The scan showed that Tim's cancer was extensive. His tongue, pallet, tonsils, larynx, jaw bone, and tissue deeper into his head were riddled with it. I explained to Tim that the odds were strong that he was going to die. I explained that the cancer had spread throughout his entire body and that treatment was not likely to work, just make his life more difficult. They were the hardest words I had ever spoken, and my already broken heart broke even more, yet Timmy looked stoic and didn't reply. I looked for words that would help this make sense to him, and to me. I wanted to be real with him, tell him the hard truth, because he trusted me and would have wanted total disclosure. I wanted to give him an opportunity to make as many decisions as he was able. I asked him if he understood that and he said he did, but his eyes clearly indicated that he wasn't really hearing me. This made it so much more difficult because I had no idea what part, if any, of this he was understanding. I was angry to be in this situation. I wanted to gather him up and protect him from all of it. I hated every word I had to speak about cancer and wanted to make all of his remaining time happy, peaceful, and comfortable.

I went on to make appointments with the oncologist, radiologist, family doctor, and palliative care doctor and to see what options were available. Charlene accompanied me to almost all the appointments. She seemed to sense the overwhelming pressure I was under and did everything she could to be there, not so much for Tim but for me. I will forever be grateful for the peace and the calmness she brought with her.

At each appointment, Tim insisted he wanted to fight for his life. I didn't want to take that away from him; none of us did. We went to see the palliative care doctors to have Tim evaluated and offered end-of-life care. If nothing else, they were going to provide him with some kick-ass pain meds. It was becoming more and more evident that further treatment would only prolong the suffering. He would still die, but it would be under much more miserable conditions.

I tried to persuade doctors to tell him that those treatments probably wouldn't work, but they said that if there was any chance at all, no matter how minute, they had to offer it as an option. I was looking for validation, something to convince Tim to turn down a treatment that would make his final days painful.

Tim insisted that he undergo radiation and chemo. He was told in the rawest details how horrible the treatments would be, but who knows if he understood. He had to stick with it; they weren't treatments you could take a break from and then go back to. He had to commit to the process entirely or quit. The radiology oncologist knew Tim would not survive and told him stories of what it would do to him. He explained that if Tim survived, he would have to have massive reconstructive surgeries on his face and jaw, he would have painful burns from the radiation and suffer through all of that, just so he could possibly live an additional month or two. Tim moved forward with the fitting for his radiation mask and his tattoo. The tattoo was given to mark where his radiation mask would go, to be certain it was lined up precisely each time he had a treatment. The schedule was beyond overwhelming. Tim had three, sometimes four appointments a day and blood work twice a week, and he would be horribly sick during all of that. He continued to pump his fist and, with his garbled speech, tried to shout "Fight!" My prayers started to sound more like begging. I had no shame when asking for guidance. I pleaded for Timmy's life. I begged God to spare him any more pain. I begged to have my mom be spared this pain. I pleaded for Tim's comfort, for all of us to see this through with strength and courage, and at the same time I cursed God for "doing" this to Timmy.

The appointments for assessment tested Tim's patience more and more as each was longer than the last and Tim became weaker and more tired. He was agitated when he had to wait too long, and I was running out of ideas to keep him calm. The physician's assistant at the oncologist's office saw me break down one day as I was scheduling more appointments. She came around the desk and gathered me up, hugged me for quite some time, and said, "I know this is difficult and I have no idea what you are going through. I just know that you are doing amazingly well." In the meantime, Tim was in the waiting room, pointing at his watch, asking me to hurry up. His patience had run out and he wanted to be home. I was feeling crushed under the weight of this responsibility. Timmy clearly did not understand what this plan of treatment meant, and I knew he would not comply. I was fighting a battle for someone not totally capable of fighting it with me. I could only push this battle to the extent of Tim's capacity, and I imagine that capacity was skewed by the voices in his head, the monsters of schizophrenia—this evil illness that had pushed him to this terminal moment in his life and left him no choice. The mental illness, not Tim, was in control. I looked at him with pleading eyes and told him that there would be days when he would be there for hours and that if he wasn't going to be patient, this wasn't going to work too well. A day or two later, Tim got into my car and handed me a restaurant gift card that he had won at work. He wanted me to have it as a thank-you for what I was doing. Sometimes, I wondered if he understood any of what was happening, and then, at that moment, I knew that he did.

Steve came home late one night to find Timmy sitting on the front porch, sound asleep with a cigarette burning a hole in his coat. The next day, I checked his coat and he had several burns. John had always had an intense fear of fire, so he started staying over at night to make sure Timmy didn't burn the house down or hurt himself. We did our best to work out a schedule so that someone could be with Tim at all times and help our mom in case something happened. Some of the family were saying to take his cigarettes away, but it was about the only thing left that he enjoyed, so I continued to buy them for him. We just had to be sure someone sat with him each time he had one.

Nicotine has incredible effects on schizophrenia. Timmy had always been a heavy smoker, and we know that this helped calm some of the psychotic symptoms. While buying cigarettes was about the last thing I wanted to do for someone suffering from cancer, I was dead set on helping him enjoy what little time he had left. Hell, I even agreed to get up at four in the morning and take him fishing, but sadly that day never came.

I showed Timmy how to use email so he could communicate with me any thoughts that might come to him at night or before I would arrive each morning. Once he mastered that, the emails would roll in, each becoming more and more bizarre.

A typical exchange of emails:

Tim: Palliet of Care: I need to get in touch with Palliet of care as soon as possible to find out if I can get something done about this infection,

Me: Are you feeling worse?

Tim: It just fills with puss how many times a day and never gets less. I think somebody told a doctor a wrong thing, that maybe I was on antibiotics too many or for too long. The antibiotics were not strong enough. palliet of care takes good care of this usually. Do you know if they will be in tomorrow?

Me: The hospital didn't find any infection. They said that puss is from the tumor inside your throat. Palliative care will talk to you more, but not until Wed. If you are having trouble breathing, 1 can get you to the hospital, but they won't give you antibiotics if the blood work shows no infection.

Tim: Yes continue Chemo And radiation for now .I am feeling better to have doctors to call and relieved to be at home and have strong enough medicine. But the syst is not better. I want you call to find out what to do

Me: Ok. Right now, the doctor wants you to use the oxycodone and put Neosporin on the cyst. Please let me know if you have any trouble breathing. I wish I could make it go away, Tim, I really do. How is the pain inside your throat and mouth? Is the oxycodone helping?

Tim: I' feeling bad a little now. Call the cancer center if you have to. I think that's wrong. Call the other doctor from cancer treatment-that woman one who talks to herself on the phone. tell her there is too much puss, like an infection. And that this sounds to strange.

Me: Tim, hang in there. I wish it was just an infection, but all of the tests show cancer and antibiotics won't help. If you want stronger medicine, I can call tomorrow and try to get them. Again, it's really important that you tell if you are breathing ok.

Tim: All I mean is I have gotten some relief the drainage on the one side and the oxycodone. The oxycodone works great and gives me much relief. on the side, there is huge hole but it has stopped draining. It gives relief to behind my head and the back of my head. The other side still drains and if drained all the way begins to show some sign of relief to around the right around the throat and throughout the whole jaw-on both sides. Thanks to the oxycodone. I just wonder what will happen if that side stops draining. They are huge holes, ugly, like the slicer hit them. So don,t worry about

it The pain is greatly less with the oxycodone. I think its gonna finish draining eventually. Don't call the doctor if you don't want to. Ill try to see if I can eat and drink more.

This last email came very late Saturday night, the night before Rich's daughter was to graduate from high school, and I let Tim know that I wouldn't see him that day. Rich's daughter had been like my own, and we had planned the graduation before we knew how sick Tim was. I would have stayed with him otherwise. I had sensed from his emails that he was becoming restless and agitated, so I called Dr. Baxter, the palliative care doctor, first thing Sunday morning and had a very long and difficult conversation with him. He was going to call in a prescription for Ativan to help Tim stay calm. Tim was insistent that he needed an antibiotic. The doctor I spoke to was truly a godsend. He was calm, sweet, and very understanding. He said that there were some very difficult decisions ahead and, either way, we would be left with some amount of guilt. Either we put Tim through treatment and live with knowing we caused him horrific suffering, or we let him die without treatment and live our lives wondering, "What if?"

I decided to lie to Tim and tell him that the doctor was calling in an antibiotic. The medication was actually Ativan to help with anxiety. We would allow Tim to believe whatever he wanted. I was crushed under the weight of what was the hardest decision I would ever make. It was clear that we would be making Timmy comfortable and waiting, painfully, for nature to take its course. I told John to take the label off the bottle and get rid of any paperwork. Tim knew what Ativan was and I didn't want him to resist taking it. Later, John texted me to tell me that Timmy refused to take the medication. He wanted to know where the paperwork was explaining what this medication was and what it did. John said he was extremely agitated and was writing notes demanding to see the paperwork. Mom even tried to give him the medication, but he politely accepted it and put it on a shelf. I called and asked to speak to Tim. I dug deep to find a lie that would work, feeling guilty all the while. I told him that since it was Sunday, they didn't have time to get all the paperwork together and that the doctor got this medication as a favor to hold him over. I told him it was a very strong antibiotic. After I hung up, John texted me and said Tim had taken the pill.

Chapter IX

Treatment

You are so brave and quiet I forget you are suffering.
~Ernest Hemmingway, *A Farewell to Arms*~

With Timmy now insisting that this was an infection, I thought it was time to contact the entire family and get everyone on the same page regarding his home treatment. With his attitude, there was no way he was going commit to chemo and radiation, which is what we all wanted. After we all agreed it was best to keep him at home with hospice care, I picked up the phone and made the hardest call of my life. I called palliative care and asked that Timmy be switched to hospice care. That way, we could keep Timmy at home and give him and the rest of us the support we needed. The doctor agreed.[8] I then called each of his doctors and canceled treatments and future appointments. I didn't want to give up on Timmy, but there was no saving his life. The greatest gift any of us could give him was to help him find comfort and finally have peace.

A few hours after cancelling all Tim's appointments, the doctor I had argued with while Tim was in the hospital called me. I was almost

---

8. "Hospice: A program designed to provide palliative care and emotional support to the terminally ill in a home or homelike setting so that quality of life is maintained, and family members may be active participants in care." Merriam-Webster Dictionary

certain he was going to lecture me and let me believe I made a bad decision. It was quite the opposite. He told me that, as a doctor, he couldn't have told me how to proceed and would not have been able to turn anyone away. But, he said Timmy would never have survived treatment and would have died in pain. Putting him through treatment would have made his last days on this earth absolutely hellish. I really needed to hear a doctor say those words and tell me that we were doing the right thing. I had the life of my brother in my hands, and I desperately needed validation that I was doing what was best, what was merciful, that which would give Tim the most quality of life in the short time he had left. I was truly grateful for that phone call. I now felt more confident moving forward with hospice care.

After the hospice nurse came in to do her evaluation, we hid all the paperwork from Timmy. All of it said "HOSPICE" in very big letters across the top, and he would certainly know what that meant. We thought it best not to tell him. He was so heavily medicated that he typically didn't even know what day it was. We were told that it was impossible to predict a timeframe for his passing because Timmy was young, just fifty-one. Even though he was so terribly sick, his body was still very strong, considering. I was contacted by the hospice social worker who became a great source of comfort for all of us. When she visited, she sat and listened to my mom and me. We shared stories of Tim's childhood. Mom smiled looking back at his innocence, and I filled in the more recent years. The social worker was there for us, and the nurse was there for Timmy.

As the days passed, it became increasingly difficult for everyone. A typical day had me getting up early, calling to check on Timmy, and then driving the thirty miles to Mom's house as quickly as I could. Timmy couldn't really speak anymore, but we sat for hours in silence, and I enjoyed every second of my time with him and our new, unique way of communicating through notes and gestures. As painful as it was to watch, I felt honored to have these moments with him that I will never have again. I helped him crush medicine and put it through his feeding tube. Each day we might try one or two possible edibles such as Jell-O or pudding to see if he could swallow anything. He reached a point where he wasn't even swallowing saliva. With the increased doses of oxycodone, he slept a lot.

In the late afternoon, John usually came by. Sometimes, we ordered a pizza, but we always ate out on the front porch. None of us had the heart to eat anything in front of Timmy, especially pizza, which was one of his favorites. We didn't even bring it inside the house for fear that the smell would be too cruel. Once we knew Timmy was settled and comfortable, we went over to the local tavern and had a beer while we recapped the day's events. I then went back to Mom's, made sure Timmy took whatever medication he needed for the evening, set up more medication in case he needed it in the middle of the night, and went home. Around 9:00 p.m., I called again to check on things.

The next day, we did it all again, after hours at home pleading with God to help him. I was growing less patient in my time of prayer, becoming accusatory and angry, blaming God for the suffering of my sweet brother, who never, not for one day, ever deserved this. I knew my prayers were in vain and there were likely no answers. If he was to pass, please, God, let it be before the suffering became too much to bear. These internal arguments with God led to more anger and pain. I was doubting that a merciful God even existed. In fact, I felt certain that He had deserted us.

Timmy took long, deep naps. I sat next to him, holding his hand, watching his chest rise and fall. Sometimes, his breathing stopped all together and then abruptly started again. One Thursday, I was certain he wouldn't wake up, so I called the family and asked them to come to the house. My mom called the church, and they sent a priest, who was also a very good friend of hers, to give Timmy his last rights. We were devastated and fought through our tears to say what we wanted him to hear last from all of us. That night around midnight, Steve texted to tell me that Timmy was up and doing laundry. We hadn't learned yet that this was to be expected. Sleep apnea is normal with terminal patients and tends to increase as they come closer to the end of their lives.

Tim continued going outside to smoke at night, and he continued to fall asleep with lit cigarettes. I often had to wake him up to keep him from burning himself. On a few occasions, I took the cigarette away from him. It was heart-crushing to watch a man with so much pride become so helpless. If there was anything to be thankful for, it was that he was so heavily medicated that he was unaware of what was happening. During one of his afternoon cigarette breaks, he told me he was having strange dreams. I asked if he had been seeing Mark and Dad as I had heard that people close to death often see their deceased loved ones. He said yes. This was both a comfort and a jab to the heart. I felt Tim's time was close.

That same weekend, on Saturday night, Tim was trying to tell John something, but John couldn't understand. John called me and said something about Tim's feeding tube. It didn't sound as if it made a whole lot of sense, and I know Tim's communication with others was not clear, so I asked them to wait until Sunday morning. When I got there Sunday morning, Tim's feeding tube had fallen out. He was still losing weight and the muscle breakdown caused the hole for the feeding tube to expand, so the tube was no longer secure. Once the tube was out, we were advised not to try and reinsert it ourselves as this was a surgical procedure. There was now no way for him to get nourishment. The hospice nurse said we could have him taken to the hospital, but in order to insert the feeding tube, they probably would have to do a tracheotomy, which would only extend the suffering and likely prohibit him from coming home. I asked Tim if he was hungry, and he shook his head and said no. After speaking with the doctor, the nurse increased his dose of pain medication, and we all waited with broken hearts. The cancer was winning. It was clear that Timmy was either going to suffocate or starve to death, and there was nothing any of us could do.

Timmy had been going upstairs to bed at night, but we were becoming increasingly concerned because he was so unsteady on his feet. We had to be careful because if Tim died from an injury, his final moments would be far worse than if he died from the cancer. There would also be implications after his death. We were told that if Tim were to die at home from the cancer, hospice would call the funeral home and together they would complete the death certificate. The process would be simple. However, if Tim were to fall and have a life-threatening injury, we would have to call 911. The nurse said that because of where his tumor was, alongside his carotid artery, any fall would cause Timmy to bleed out. The aftermath would look like a murder scene and be too much for all of us to witness, especially Mom. Tim would be taken to the hospital and they would do what they could to save his life, which would likely cause even more trauma for him. Then, if he were to die from those injuries, an autopsy would have to be performed and the death certificate process would take much longer.

So, we had hospice order a hospital bed to be put on the main floor in the den where Timmy spent almost all his time. We bought new sheets and pillows and made it look as close as possible to his own bed. Tim just looked at it and laid down on the couch. As I said, he trusted no one, yet, somehow, he would do anything I told him. I explained that the bed was in the living room so he could be comfortable downstairs and visitors could use the couch. I told him the bed would be a whole lot more comfortable than the couch. He walked over, tested it with his hand, and climbed right in.

His breathing now seemed even worse than before. When he slept, there were long periods where he did not breathe at all. The hospice nurse wanted to transition him from oxycodone to a morphine pump but had to do that gradually. The doctor also added Haldol, an antipsychotic drug that is often prescribed for restlessness in patients who are terminally ill. All the medication was now being dosed through a syringe that I put under his tongue. I had to write down every time he needed that medication and give him the morphine every hour on the hour, or more often if needed. I stayed over the night the hospital bed was delivered, as did John. It was the longest night I can remember.

Timmy's loyalty to our mom would have kept him fighting forever as he felt a profound sense of responsibility to care for her. I knew it was important for him to hear from her that she would be okay and that he was free to let go. I asked her to tell him it was okay to die. The hardest part of that night was watching Mom sit with him, gently take his hand, and through her tears, assure him that she would be okay. She asked him to follow Mark and Dad and have peace. I don't believe I have ever been so heartbroken in all my life. My eighty-five-year-old mother, who had already had to bury her oldest son, was now telling her youngest son it was okay to die. It called to mind the many times I held my own son's hand and encouraged him to take a next step, whether I was giving a first-day-of-school pep talk or a pregame chat to calm his nerves. It was unfathomable to think that I would be telling him to let go of this life and say goodbye. That was one of many times when I cursed God and questioned why our merciful God allowed a beautiful soul to suffer like this. Why does anyone suffer? Why does cancer even exist? I was so angry, and somewhere between my anger and my tears, my belief in anything good ceased. All I could see was my beautiful brother, reduced to a few pounds of bone and flesh, being tortured by voices only he could hear, afraid of those who were there to help him, and now suffering as cancer literally destroyed him from the inside out. It all seemed so insulting, and even as I write, I am angry. Why? Why Timmy? Why my eighty-five-year-old mother? Why any of us? I begged that, if there was a God, for Him to please show mercy and give Tim peace. For Christ's sake, he suffered far too long as it was! Why would God allow this for one more minute?

Timmy continually got up throughout the night and was clearly hallucinating. He insisted on going outside to smoke. He didn't even have a cigarette in his hand anymore. He just went through the motions. I had to hold him as he walked because he was so frail and unsteady. I had my alarm set for every hour to be sure to give Tim his morphine; however, I never needed it. Every time I was almost asleep, Timmy would get up. He wanted to use the upstairs bathroom, but I wouldn't allow it because of how unsteady he was on his feet. I made him use the half bath that was down on the main level. He had been in there a while and came out handing me a tube of toothpaste. I giggled and he smiled a sly smile that told me there was something going on in his mind to which I was not privy. I took the toothpaste and thanked him as I helped him back to his bed. Nothing he did that night made much sense. Finally, when morning came, John took over and I ran home to shower. In addition to all that was happening, my car had broken down and I was using John's to run home. I rushed back to Mom's and Charlene met me there. Timmy was completely out of it. He was holding his sneaker up to his mouth as though he were drinking from it. He moved his hands as though he were smoking. We had given him so much morphine and Haldol, yet he was still restless and, even when lying down, his legs and feet were in constant motion. It was hard to see him going through this, but I was grateful for the drugs that made him unaware and helped him feel less pain. I put on quiet, soothing music, and we just waited.

Late morning, Thursday, June 18, 2015, exactly one month and one day after our initial trip to the hospital, Timmy finally settled in and looked like he would sleep. I noticed his breathing was shallower and more intermittent than before. Somehow, I felt that today was going to be the day. I sat with Tim and told him that I had kept my promise to be his advocate, and now I needed him to make me a promise. I told him that he should rest. I explained how I knew how strong and brave he had been to have endured all that he had and that he was, and will always be, my big brother, my hero. I said that when he saw Mark and Dad, he should go with them and have peace from all of his demons. I assured him the love I had for him was eternal and that he earned his wings to fly away from this place and this suffering. He nodded his head and promised he would.

Kathy, the social worker, had called to ask if she could come by. I had also called Timmy's nurse and asked her to come. Between Charlene and me, we contacted the rest of the family and asked that they come. Jimmy was travelling on business but had said goodbye over the weekend and instructed Timmy not to wait for him. Dennis had come by on his lunch break and called work to let them know he would not be back that day, and John was already there. Steve came and Charlene sat with Kathy and Mom in the living room as the rest of us were with Tim in the back room. My mom was well aware of what was happening but seemed to be in a state of shock, knowing that the day had finally arrived. The day she had feared, dreaded, and prayed for a miracle to interrupt. She was facing unimaginable pain and none of us will ever know what she was truly feeling.

Once everyone was there, it seemed Timmy knew we were together for him, to say goodbye. Just around 1:30, Timmy started convulsing as if gasping for air. I sat on the bed with him, one hand over his heart and the other holding his hand. He had been throwing his legs and one ended up around my waist. I fought tears and kept telling him how much I loved him and that it was okay to go. For two hours Tim faded in and out. I kept reminding him of his promise, to let go and not fight it. At one point, while John was at the foot of the bed, Tim's eyes opened, and a huge smile came across his face. It lasted only a second, but it left us with no doubt that he saw something amazing. John, in almost a falsetto voice, said, "He just saw where he is going, he just saw where he is going. Go there, Tim, go."

Other than that brief smile, Tim's experience of his last moments seemed so disruptive, not like when people say, "He went peacefully." No, there was nothing peaceful about this. I had given him another dose of morphine to be certain he wasn't feeling any of it. I can't recall just how much morphine I had given him, but it no longer seemed important to be strictly measuring; it was only important to keep him from experiencing any discomfort. I could just barely feel his heart; it was almost stopped. Suddenly, Abby, the family dog, who was sitting on Dennis' lap, started to purr. It was a sound like no one had ever heard before and especially strange coming from a dog. We all stopped to listen, and she did it again with her head up and looking to the ceiling, and then she gently whimpered. Only a minute later, Timmy was free. The suffering had finally ended. Timmy was whole again. No voices, no cancer, just freedom.

I feel quite certain that Timmy's soul passed through me as it left this world. He was and always will be a part of me, a part of all I do, and he will live on forever in my heart. I don't know that I have ever loved another human being quite as much as I loved Timmy. My heart is broken. I am broken.

Chapter X
It's Time

Death ends a life, not a relationship.
~Mitch Albom, *Tuesdays With Morrie*~

The quiet in the house soon ended with the hustle and bustle of the nurse and me getting rid of all the medications. Then, the nurse and Kathy, the social worker, prepared Tim's body for viewing so we could say goodbye one more time and the funeral directors could come and take him. I called Rich a few times, but he was unable to answer. When he was able, he called right away, knowing that three missed calls from me must have meant something important. He rushed to my mom's as quickly as possible. As Dennis was taking something to his car, one of the neighbors, Terence, who had no idea what was going on, said a friendly, "Hello and how are you?" Dennis told him that our brother had just died. Terence came right to the house, gathered my mom up in his arms, and wept. He knew that she had already lost a son and was heartbroken for her to have lost another. A few minutes later, a neighbor from across the street came over to say hello; she had no idea that Tim had died. I think everyone was shocked. He had only been diagnosed four weeks earlier. Things had happened so quickly in retrospect, but it felt like an eternity while we were watching him. Time really does slow down. It was painful each day, but we also had each day.

I had the most precious and valuable time with him. We laughed, I cried, we sat in silence, we shared a Guinness, and we wrote notes. I got to tell him everything I ever wanted to say, and I knew that I left nothing for regret.

After Rich arrived, the Finegans were close behind. The Finegans were the funeral directors responsible for all the McNally funerals. They are Irish and that means a lot to my mom. They had handled my dad's funeral, and since my mom was a soloist for funerals at her church, she came to know them very well. When the Finegans arrived, Rich and the brothers helped take Timmy's body out the back door so Mom could stay in the living room and not have to see. I stayed with her as did Kathy. I am still not sure if Mom had come to grips yet with what had happened. I don't think she had digested any of it and probably wouldn't until the smoke cleared and she was alone. John had decided to continue to stay with her at night. We were all afraid of the effect Tim's death would have on her. I remember saying, months earlier, that if Timmy died, she would likely go soon after. They relied on each other. They had a relationship that no one will ever fully understand and which has no definition. Theirs truly fit into the unconditional love category.

Once things settled, Charlene poured everyone a Guinness and, as a good Irish family should, we drank a toast to the beautiful soul that had just left this world: "Goodbye Timmy. May you live on forever in peace and wholeness. We love you." On the way home from my mom's, Rich went into rescue mode but, as an only child who had never lost anyone, had no idea how to empathize with me. He insisted we stop to eat, which I was not the least bit interested in doing. I was ill at ease the entire time we spent in the restaurant. I couldn't focus on where I was or why I was there. I didn't know where I wanted to be; I just knew I didn't want to be there. I felt like I had no business sitting down to a nice dinner after what I had just witnessed, after what Timmy had just gone through. How dare I do something comforting. I felt as though I should be suffering just to make it right. As much time as I'd had to prepare, as much time as I'd had to say everything I wanted to say, it just didn't matter. He was gone, he suffered, it was horrible, and I was crushed. There was no comfort to be found.

The next morning, I returned to Mom's. John and I tried to make coffee, only to find that during a drug-induced stupor, Timmy had filled the reservoir of the coffee maker with powdered nondairy creamer. As hard as we tried, we could not clean it all out. It was as if Timmy had wanted one last laugh! We chuckled to imagine what he must have been thinking.

The family later regrouped to make funeral arrangements. My nephew Andrew would be making the trip from Kansas; a friend of my mother's came to go over readings and music for the church; and Jimmy, John, Steve, and I met at the funeral home. We worked together to write the obituary and made a quick selection of the casket. There had been much debate over whether there was room in the family plot. We originally thought that there was room for only one, which would be for Mom. We had asked her if Timmy could be cremated and then have his ashes buried with her when her time came. I think that thought was difficult for a Catholic mother. Cremation had not been honored by the church, and although it was acceptable now, it wasn't something she believed in. After some more investigation, we found out that there were actually two graves left. This meant so much to our mom: Tim would not be cremated, and they would still be buried together as she had wanted.

We continued with interment plans. We laughed, we cried, and we loved as we made the final arrangements. Jimmy had been working on the eulogy (he is the actual writer in the family). Mom stayed home and was comforted by friends who dropped by, cards that flooded the mailbox, and flowers that were delivered. She tried to keep track of everything so she could properly thank everyone who thought of her and all of us. It was overwhelming.

That day and the days to follow both moved in slow motion and flew past. I know that sounds crazy, but it seemed never-ending and now, looking back, it was a flash. One person's entire life was to be summed up and finalized in a matter of days. From where do those customs arise, and why do we keep them? It's painful and although some say those rituals are necessary, they put you into a function mode that is almost unreal. We ran around planning the funeral, planning the luncheon to follow, planning everything, yet taking very little time to face the horrible pain that was eating each and every one of us. Timmy was gone and, yes, no longer in pain, but he was gone, and life will never be the same. I would really like to wake up now.

Timothy T. McNally Obituary

Timothy T. McNally, 51, of Easton, Pa., passed away peacefully at his home, surrounded by his loving family. He was born on December 21, 1963, in Easton. Tim was the son of the late Francis M. McNally, Sr., and Joan M. Harrison McNally. Tim worked for CIGNA in Easton. He was a loving caretaker to his mother, avid fisherman, avid Dead Head and a lifelong Buffalo Bills fan, although that is not what took his life. Tim was a member of Our Lady of Mercy Parish, Easton. Tim is survived by his mother, Joan M. Harrison McNally of Easton; he is also survived by his siblings: Stephen J. McNally of Easton, John K. McNally of Bethlehem Twp., James C. McNally and his wife M. Charlene of Bushkill Twp., Dennis P. McNally of Plainfield Twp., Mary Kate McNally and her companion Rich of Alburtis, Pa., his nephews, Andrew C. McNally and Sean H. Thorman, and his niece Kathryn A. McNally. Tim was predeceased by his father Francis M. McNally, Sr., and his brother Francis M. McNally, Jr. Funeral services will begin at 9:00 a.m. on Thursday, June 25, 2015, at The Finegan Funeral Home, 4080 William Penn Highway, Palmer Twp., followed by a Funeral Mass at 10:00 a.m. at St. Bernard's Oratory, 132 S. 5th St. Easton, Pa. Calling hours will be held on Wednesday, June 24, 2015, from 6:00 to 8:00 p.m. in the funeral home. Interment will take place in Holy Saviour Cemetery,

Bethlehem. In lieu of flowers, Memorials may be made to St. Luke's

Cancer Center, 1872 St. Luke's Blvd., Easton, Pa. 18045 or Our Lady of Mercy – St. Bernard's Oratory, 132 S. 5th St., Easton, Pa. 18042.

Wednesday, June 24, 2015, the day of the viewing, I woke up with severe pain in my left foot. I have no memory of having done anything to it; I was just in pain. Rich tried to rub my foot, yet that only seemed to make it worse. No matter, I had things to do. Rich's daughter and I had run out to get dress pants and a shirt for him to wear both to the viewing and to the funeral. None of his dress clothes fit anymore, and I didn't feel jeans were appropriate. After dropping off Rich's clothes, I got dressed and went to John's house, which was right down the street from the funeral home. Rich, his mother, and daughter had planned to drive separately and come a bit later. The rest of the family had decided to meet at John's and then go to the viewing together. Jimmy and Charlene parked in the back at the funeral home and had coolers filled with beer and wine. I was thrilled to see that we were doing this in the proper "Irish wake" fashion. I was having trouble walking as my foot was getting worse. I had on three-inch heels that seemed to actually alleviate the pain—until I took them off. Being flat on my feet was excruciating. I understand calling hours, but I don't understand viewings. I am always so touched by the outpouring of love and support and will forever be grateful for that time to know how much my brother meant to so many others. I guess I just don't get the body's being on display. This was certainly not Timmy any longer. Timmy was free, and this was the body that trapped him in sickness for so long. I would prefer to close the casket and have pictures of him when he was smiling and well. We did have pictures, but the body on display I will never understand.

Well over one hundred people came. Friends, family, former neighbors, former coworkers, friends of friends. It was a lot to take in. At one point, a huge group came in together. They were all of Timmy's coworkers. The boss had closed the office for a few hours so they could all come and say goodbye. It still amazes me how close they all were. We had no idea of the life Timmy'd had at work. Our hearts overflowed with peace, knowing he was loved so much more than we had ever known. After two hours, we headed out to a family dinner before saying goodnight. The next day would be long and painful, and we all knew it.

Thursday came quickly and with very little sleep. I could not walk at all because my foot had gotten so bad. It was swollen and turning purple. I could not put any weight on it. Rich was insisting that I go get it checked, but I vehemently declined. Today was Timmy's funeral. I was doing one of the readings, and I didn't care if the damn thing fell off, I was going to go and say goodbye. It took everything I had to shower and get dressed. I texted my brothers to ask for crutches; in the meantime, Rich acted as my crutch as he helped me out to my car. John met me at the car with crutches when I arrived at our mom's. All the while, in my head, I was pleading, "Dear God, please get us through this day." Taking our mother to the funeral of another child was about as much hell as any of us could imagine. It was unfair, cruel; she surely did not deserve this. I had now become an authority on who deserves what, or so I thought. Soon, the limousine pulled up to take us to the funeral home. We had another calling for an hour before the funeral. Several more friends came and then we had a private prayer with just the family before going to the church.

Father Keith, who had come to give Timmy his final blessing, was out of the country. My mom was disappointed that he would not be saying the Mass, but the priest who had visited every day in the hospital would. He was from South Africa, so his English was broken and at times hard to understand. Somehow, that didn't matter. We were all in so much pain that I'm not sure any of us really listened.

It was time for me to do my reading. It was one I had chosen and had always been my favorite. I hobbled my way to the alter, bowed, and made my way to the ambo (podium). I tried desperately to grab each word, understand it, get it, feel it, and deliver it.

A reading from Ecclesiastes, 3:-There is a time for everything, and a season for every activity under the heavens: A time to be born and a time to die, A time to plant and a time to uproot,

A time to kill and a time to heal, A time to tear down and a time to build, A time to weep and a time to laugh, A time to mourn and a time to dance, A time to scatter stones and a time to gather them, A time to embrace and a time to refrain from embracing, A time to search and a time to give up, A time to keep and a time to throw away, A time to tear and a time to mend, A time to be silent and a time to speak, A time to love and a time to hate, A time for war and a time for peace.

I believed all those words, yet they felt empty at the time. I understood there was a time to die; I just didn't understand why this was the time and why it was Timmy who had to go. I know I seem pretty arrogant in expecting so many answers. I suppose it was just a part of mourning. It was time to mourn.

My niece Katie and nephew Andrew did readings as well. Then it was Jimmy's turn. We all had our tissues ready, as we had sat through two other eulogies he had written, and they were more poignant than anything.

Timothy Thomas McNally (12/21/63 – 6/18/15)

—as written by Jimmy McNally

I'm Jim McNally, Tim's brother. For those without a scorecard, and in memory of our Dad, the "batting order," as he loved to call it, is as follows:

Our beloved, late brother Mark, is number one.Number two is Steve.

Number three is John.I'm number four.Number five is Dennis.Our dear Timmy, is number six.

And last, but most certainly not least, is Mary Kate, the only girl: number seven.

My family, knowing so painfully as we do, Timmy's thirty-year battle with a terribly cruel affliction, doesn't wish to celebrate his difficult life so much as we wish to celebrate his beautiful release: his new life in heaven, free from pain and torment; finally, at peace. To our family, Timmy was like a gentle lamb. He was so

innocent. He never caused harm to anyone. And despite having some terrible wrongs and a devastating disease visited upon him, his heart never hardened. He was never bitter. He always put others first. His kindness had no limit. That was our Timmy.

Many years ago, in a short period of relative clarity, Tim was deeply remorseful and apologetic for what he thought he'd put us through while we struggled to help him. It broke our hearts.

Timmy, please know that you were never a burden. You are the most courageous person we've ever known. You were an inspiration. You ARE an inspiration. You inspire us to be kinder and more caring—like you. You inspire us to hold no bitterness, to be forgiving, and to love each other, more dearly—like you. You inspire us to be more faithful—like

you. You embodied the Holy Spirit and the faith and values instilled in you by Mom and Dad, at home and in this church. Our family has never been closer, more loving to each other, stronger in faith, and as prayerful. That is what you left behind, Timmy. We want you to know that. Please know that.

Timmy was the fourth of our "Irish quadruplets," born in consecutive years from 1960 to 1963. He had those penetrating blue eyes. He had lighter hair and was taller and better looking than the rest of us. He was the baby of the family for four years and Mary Kate recalls how he was reluctant to surrender that special spot on Dad's knee, eventually agreeing to share the other knee with his new baby sister. Dad loved it. And it was the start of a special bond between Kate and Timmy that lasted until he took his last breath, with her hand on his chest to feel his last heartbeat.

Above all things, Timmy was a gentle, loving, Christian soul whose treatment of others is a model for us. Secondly, he honored his mother and father and was a loving caretaker to Mom, even as he struggled with his disease. Their relationship was a tender and beautiful love story. He lived with Mom until the end. He did her shopping, brought home her favorite meals, ran errands, shared glasses of wine, and always made certain she was looked after. He never denied her a single request. We all have big shoes to fill in that regard. And Tim nodded and was pleased each time we assured him we would.

Timmy was extraordinarily intelligent and insightful. He was very quiet and thoughtful and deep. Tim was an avid

fisherman, and several friends, in their condolences, mentioned happy times spent fishing with him. Tim loved the Yankees in baseball, and the Buffalo Bills in football, as if he needed any more heartbreak in his life.

He was a gifted athlete who excelled in baseball and basketball. He could cover an entire outfield from his position in center. He made the entire infield look good with his saving plays at first base. I recall countless hours playing one-on-one basketball with Timmy. I'd try to run circles around him with my speed, and he'd just shoot over top of me and never give up a rebound. He made me a better outside shooter.

Tim enjoyed a variety of music, especially The Grateful Dead, an acquired taste, for sure. But one he shared with several of his siblings. Tim and I listened to many hours of the Dead and attended several concerts together. Their songs will always remind us of good times spent with Tim. So many roads. So many roads.

Tim was a reliable and trusted co-worker for more than twenty years at Cigna. It's unlikely they knew the extent of Tim's struggles. But we've been overwhelmed by his co-workers' touching expressions of sympathy. Tim was part of team that was a family at Cigna and it's clear they truly loved him. We're so comforted they came to know our Tim as we did: gentlemanly, thoughtful, trustworthy, reliable, and always helpful.

Tim was a mysterious uncle to Andrew, Kate, and Sean, who were too young to understand the mystery but now know the depth of his character and the love he had for them and all of us. They didn't know him well. But they loved him as much as we all did.

Steve remembers simple pleasures, like Tim calling next door over the old house-to-house intercom to invite Sean and him out to eat. Sean was always thrilled to stay up late and be out with the big boys.

Mom remembers his innocence when asking Timmy about his first day of school. When he mentioned they sang songs, Mom asked if they sang with the piano. He replied matter-of-factly, with his long-gone lisp, "No. We just sang with our 'mouthes.'"

John remembers Tim's subtle yet hilarious sense of humor, a trait surely inherited from Dad. Tim's first car was a huge old Buick Electra he bought from a lifelong friend of Dad. At some point the car developed electrical gremlins that strangely caused the horn to honk whenever the steering wheel was turned. One day, John could hear

Timmy's car horn for blocks as he was maneuvering and making turns while driving home. The horn honking built to a noisy crescendo as he parallel parked in front of the house. John was nearly in tears laughing when Tim got out of the car and calmly asked, "Do you know of any weddings in the area this weekend?"

I remember delivering newspapers with Tim. We played on the same baseball team a couple of years. I remember the glorious day our Sullivan Park softball team won the city championship with several McNallys in the lineup, including Tim in center field, of course. What a team! We worked together at the Brewers' Outlet, the old beer store in town. I remember my best friend, my best man, my son's godfather. I recall how we stayed up all night talking and celebrating and sharing such happiness on the night Andrew was born. It was one of the best moments of my life, and Timmy wanted all the details and couldn't hear enough about it. I'll never forget that night as long as I live.

Dennis shared a bedroom and strong bond with his closest sibling. There was that memorable day when Dad took Dennis and Timmy to a Lafayette football game. The rules were simple. Stay close to Dad and don't wander off. My brothers and I were playing football at Sullivan Park, just a couple blocks away where you could easily monitor the game by the public address announcements and the roar of the crowd. Suddenly, public address announcer Jim Finnen came on the loudspeakers and said, "From the lost and found department, we have two boys looking for their dad. Will Mr. McNally please report to press box to retrieve Dennis and Tim." While it makes for a great story now, none of us wanted to be home when Dad returned with them. Dennis always looked after Tim, sometimes to a fault. Our family had strict neighborhood boundaries, based upon age, that were not permitted to be crossed. For young Timmy and Dennis, one of them was the alley off Hamilton Street. One day, Timmy decided to cross the alley, despite Dennis's screaming admonishments delivered while jumping up and down in panic. Dennis looked both ways several times, jumped across the alley, grabbed Timmy's arm and sunk his teeth into it for disciplinary purposes. All of this was witnessed by our neighbor and Mom's friend Mrs. Rute, who could barely relate the story over the phone because she was laughing so hard at Dennis's special brand of brotherly love for Tim. When I asked Dennis, last weekend, if that taught Timmy to behave, Dennis pondered for a few seconds and said, "I don't think he ever did anything wrong after that for the rest of his life."

Mary Kate remembers Timmy writing scripts for her to follow when they made prank phone calls on Friday and Saturday nights. Nothing mean; it was more of the "Prince Albert in a can" variety. They were simpler, happier times that would forge the strongest bond any of us had with Timmy. Timmy chose wisely. He confided in her and trusted her with his life—quite literally. In his final weeks, Mary Kate went from being the baby of the family to our spiritual and emotional leader. We all have guardian angels and Timmy's walks among us in the person of Mary Kate. She promised him she'd protect him from harm and not let him be put through unnecessary pain. He promised her he'd go with the angels and Mark and Dad when they came to take him to heaven. They kept their promises.

Because of Timmy, our hearts are filled with gratitude for the angels who sent messages, or called, or visited, or passed briefly through our lives at different times during those last weeks. To Tim's medical caretakers—doctors, nurses, social workers—to his thoughtful co-workers, and his old friends, we thank you. To all our family who have become friends, and our friends who have become family, we thank you. To Father Keith who administered Anointing of the Sick and called to check on Mom, thank you. To Father Elias, who exhibited such compassion and kept us in good humor when he visited with us in the hospital to pray with Tim, we thank you. To the beautiful choirs of this parish and all its wonderful members who are such a source of strength for

Mom, we thank you. My old pastor, Fr. Sheehan, always reminded us that sung prayers are heard twice. We appreciate your double duty. Again, thank you.

Timmy was baptized in this church. He was an altar boy here. It's so appropriate that he's come back here to make his final journey, in this beautiful church that is the rock upon which our family is built—and has been for more than fifty-five years. Thank you, St. Bernard's. Thank you, Our Lady of Mercy.

We're comforted by so many friends who've shared their condolences at the "loss" of Timmy. But we're confident in our faith that Timmy is not lost. We believe we know exactly where he is: in heaven with Dad and Mark, sitting quietly— and, knowing them—very, very quietly.

Timmy left us peacefully, in answer to our prayers. I left on a business trip, two days prior, and was not there at the end. When we last spoke, I told him I loved him and asked him not to wait for me to return. He didn't. But he was surrounded by Mom and Steve and John and Dennis and Charlene, and of course, Mary Kate, who caressed his head and comforted him. When the angels and Mark and Dad came for him, Mom's dog Abby whimpered and stared blankly into the air. She knew they were there and could likely smell the dog treats Dad always kept in his pocket. Timmy finally smiled and we knew he was finally seeing heaven and it was beautiful. He drew his last breath and went to paradise, free from his pain and suffering and torment; his beautiful mind restored; made whole, and finally at rest with his beautiful soul.

Timmy, what you left behind is in each of us and it's a

blessing. You touched our lives in ways unimaginable: your courage, your compassion, your trust, your faith, your gentle kindness. You were never a burden. Never. You are with us always and we are stronger and more faithful because of you. Fare thee well, my brother. Rest in the peace of our loving God.

I was still on crutches, but Jimmy and I helped each other out of the church that day, collapsing into each other's arms as we walked past the casket. Hands down, this was the hardest day of either of our lives, and it wasn't over yet. We were taken to the cemetery for the final blessing, and we each walked by the casket, placed our hand on it, and said one last "I love you."

Timmy's life was both a blessing and a tragedy. This incredible soul was put to the test, and he walked with demons every day. He smiled, he loved, and he lived the best he knew how. I am angry and confused about how his life went and how it ended. I can't imagine feeling greater love for anyone. Timmy was ripped off in this life! A fifty-one-year-old man who never traveled. He never boarded a plane, took a vacation, met the woman of his dreams, had a home of his own, or any other "normal" thing most of us get to experience. He was slighted, denied a fair life. I can't imagine feeling a stronger drive to make it right. I promised I would be his voice, and yes, he's gone, but as his voice, I live on. I will go to the ends of the earth to tell his story, to brag about his bravery and raise him up, always. Timmy's life mattered. Timmy's life still matters.

There are millions of men and women suffering from mental illness who will never seek medical help. They feel the stigma that goes with being mentally ill. They feel ashamed or alone or so overwhelmed by voices that they don't feel they can get help. There are families struggling with a mentally ill member and they are at a total loss as to what to do. We need help. We need help that is bigger than all of us.

This fucking monstrous disease caused him to mistrust the people who loved him endlessly and would never, ever hurt him. God damn it! Timmy was ripped off in this life and I'm pissed as hell about it! We have so many laws in place to protect the privacy of patients, which is both a blessing and a curse. If the barriers could have been a little less stringent, we could possibly have received a call from Tim's employer to let us know he had not turned in his insurance renewal forms. We might have heard from the dentist that something was seriously wrong and that

Timmy needed our intervention sooner. The emergency room doctor could have contacted us that Thanksgiving night to direct us, but alas, we protect each other, quite literally, to death.

Since Timmy's passing, I have moved to Arizona. My mother has been hospitalized several times and spends her days longing for Timmy. The mourning never ends, and it doesn't get easier. It simply gets different. In moments when we are enjoying life and taking pleasure in something like a Grateful Dead song, Timmy will come to mind, and the tears will start to flow. He is in every single day and I wouldn't change that fact, ever. "Fare thee well, fare thee well, I love you more than words can tell…" (The Grateful Dead, "Fare Thee Well")

Chapter XI
Fare Thee Well

Mental illness is nothing to be ashamed of, but stigma and bias shame us all.
~Bill Clinton~

I f you know of someone or are a family member of someone who is mentally ill, I urge you to please step forward. Break down the stigma that surrounds mental illness. There are so many groups that are lobbying for new laws and offering support to loved ones. I only learned of those things after Timmy was issued his death sentence. It doesn't have to be that way. Our country desperately needs change in this field. We have mentally ill people behind bars when they should be receiving medical treatment. The homeless rate of mentally ill is beyond measure and must be changed. Timmy was one of the fortunate ones who had a family that would never give up on him. Sadly, not all families are able to cope, and they bow out of the lives of their mentally ill member.

If your family member had diabetes or cancer, surely you would not turn your back on them. Mental illness is no different. It is nothing to be ashamed about. If the proper laws were in place, we could all intercede and take over guardianship of adults with mental illnesses. Providing them with healthcare would be so much simpler and we, as families who feel the heartache, would have more say in their care, knowing their dignity is being preserved. And we'd be able to sleep at night, knowing they are safe.

Thank you for taking the time to read this story. I hope that it touches you in a way that will change your view of the mentally ill, and I urge you to get involved and make a difference.

www.ingramcontent.com/pod-product-compliance
Lightning Source LLC
Chambersburg PA
CBHW052012030426
42334CB00029BA/3194